SAVING
SECULAR
SOCIETY

Alive Publishing Ltd

SAVING SECULAR SOCIETY

Dudley Plunkett

First published in 2007 by Alive Publishing Ltd,
Graphic House, 124 City Road, Stoke on Trent ST4 2PH
Tel: +44 (0) 1782 745600 Fax: +44 (0) 1782 745500
e-mail:editor@biblealive.co.uk

Scripture texts used in this book are taken from the Revised
Standard Version Bible with Apocryphal/Deutero-canonical
Books.
Copyrighted ©1965 and 1996. Used with permission.

© 2007 Dudley Plunkett
British Library Catalogue-in-Publication Data. A catalogue
record for this book is available from the British Library.

ISBN: 978-0-9540335-5-2

AKNOWLEDGEMENTS

owe a debt of gratitude especially to the many people who have inspired me, but to none more than Pope John Paul II who constantly evoked the theme of the creative tensions between faith, reason and culture. I also thank Cardinal Paul Poupard, Presedent of the Pontifical Council for Culture, for his gracious and authoritative introduction to the book. I have benefited greatly from being able to test my ideas in conversations and seminars with my Maryvale colleagues, Fr Paul Watson, Petroc Willey, Stephen Yates and Caroline Farey. At a practical level I have learnt from many Catholic friends who share my zeal for the new evangelisation and have shown me its reality by their example. I thank all those at Alive Publishing for their enthusiasm for the work of evangelising and for their help and support in bringing this publication to a completion, and I want also to thank my wife, Francine, and my family, who have given me their encouragement and a critical but tolerant sounding-board.

Dr Dudley Plunkett, Senior Academic Tutor at the Maryvale Institute, Birmingham, studied Sociology and Education at the University of Chicago and then worked in the field of teacher education at Southampton University. He has authored several books and articles on socio-religious themes, including Secular and Spiritual Values (Routledge, 1990), Queen of Prophets: the Spiritual Message of Medjugorje (DLT, 1990), and Heaven Wants to be Heard (Gracewing, 1997). He is married, with two children and three grandchildren.

CONTENTS

FOREWORD

By Cardinal Paul Poupard

Fresh eyes, fresh hope, fresh vigour. These are the gifts the Church's engagement with contemporary culture needs in order to concretise the pastoral approach to culture that I have long been mandated to promote as President of the Pontifical Council for Culture. This is the task Dr Plunkett has set himself as he echoes many of the riches of the Church's ancient missionary tradition and draws particularly on the new evangelisation encouraged by Popes Paul VI, John Paul II and now Benedict XVI.

They too have stood on the shoulders of giants before them, disciples all of the Son of God who took on lowly human form to bring the light of truth to the entire world. By his Incarnation and persistent ministry, even unto death on a cross, he has won for us and shown us the way to salvation, leaving us with an ever-new message that fulfils and transforms men and women in their societies, creating new cultures. In the footsteps of St Paul, my patron and the greatest missionary apostle, Dr Plunkett seeks to bring that message to one area of today's Areopagus, secular culture, by challenging it with the old question, "What is truth?"

In his 2005 Christmas greeting to the members of the Roman Curia, Pope Benedict XVI underlined the importance of the Church's engagement with contemporary culture, noting that "it is a dialogue that needs to be developed with great open-mindedness, and also with clear discernment that the world rightly expects from us at this time."[1]

While it is not helpful to rant about the chronic dearth of contemporary culture—perhaps regurgitating those worn-out sayings that merely add oxygen to the flames of discouragement— endeavours such as Dr Plunkett's nevertheless need to contextualise with succinct analysis the modern field of evangelisation, i.e. secular culture.

Clearly distinguishing secularism from secularisation, and contemplating the Church's place therein with the frank and honest self-inspection that helps avoid hypocrisy, the modern apostle can then go on to raise his central theme: what the hope we have within us can offer to secular culture, and how we can help the Gospel message bring to bear its salvific effects.

One of the preferred fields for this work is that of culture; it is the battleground for the future of humanity. Through it the Church can reach out and establish dialogue with our contemporaries in terms accessible to them; by sharing the joys and hopes, fears and anxieties of men and women in contemporary cultures, the Church engages with them, and walks with them on their pilgrimage through life. At the same time as embracing cultures in this way, the Church is also counter-cultural. Taking as model the Good Samaritan, She steps out of the norm to nurture men and women in their cultures, with a process of purification, sacrifice and prayer.

Far from a simple lament about the things we disdain, ours is the task of shedding the light of truth on the current situation, baptising it where possible and mercifully helping it, not so much in a cultural clash which will see Christianity conquer secularism, but in a tender dialogue which helps contemporary cultures recover the riches of Christian Revelation, thereby permitting a further growth towards their proper fulfilment.

The Enlightenment project to make faith and reason irreconcilable has now failed, although the vocal minority of secularists does receive undue attention in our dialectic world. Instead, the contemporary dilemma has more to do with indifference, relativism, insecurity and confusion, leading to a general loss of anchor points to transmit the faith from one generation to the next.

While faith and reason are not opposed, contemporary hearts are often closed to them by countless distractions. What is needed—and Dr Plunkett echoes this call—is to make secular culture reopen its horizons, make it face the big questions, restore the human quest for truth, and open a window for the actions of grace. This is the response to the trend of contemporary culture to ignore faith and the truth. This is the eagle which soars on the two wings of faith and reason.

For some, the concepts of Inculturation, Redemption, Resurrection and Pentecost may seem abstract notions and a far cry from the pragmatic questions and real issues people face locally and daily. But these are the very foundations of salvation and of the pastoral approach to culture, which seeks to stimulate men and women in their cultures to seek fulfilment.

Energy, courage and insight are required to find the anchor points and concrete tools to establish dialogue with non-believers and open their hearts to these truths. A recent publication by the Pontifical Council for Culture, *Where is Your God?* gathered together different practical propositions, concentrating on the centrality of prayer and the human person, the personal nature of dialogue, the Church's presence in the public square, the role of the family, school and catechesis, the stimulation of beauty and use of emotions, the opportunities of Catholic Cultural Centres, etc. Some of the seven steps suggested by Dr Plunkett reflect those priorities.

Finally, it remains for me to wish the author and reader new courage as they Cast out into the Deep, responding to that divine command in the wake of the first fishermen who replied 'At your Word Lord, I will cast the nets', for even in secular culture people thirst for something that truly satisfies—that is the nature of being human.

What we can offer is the Saviour of the World, who lets us become more human, and indeed become more alike to Christ. Such is our salvation.

[1] Benedict XVI, Address to the Roman Curia, 22 December 2005, in *L'Osservatore Romano* Weekly English Edition, N.1 (1925), 4 January 2006, p.4.

INTRODUCTION

Can Secular Society find Hope?

ECULAR SOCIETY IS facing great uncertainties and challenges, whether we are thinking of values in everyday life, ethics in political and scientific decision-making, criteria for beauty in the arts and art criticism, or integrity in broadcasting. Perplexity about these issues has led many to adopt the stance of ironical spectator, iconoclastic artist, or some other anarchic or despairing response like youthful vandalism. But what if such negativity were to be rejected? What if people could more courageously face the challenge of living with each other in a positive attitude of acceptance, caring and community? The thesis of this book is that this positive vision for humanity has always existed in the Judaeo-Christian tradition, and even though it has often appeared lost, or has been temporarily overshadowed, it is time for it to be renewed.

A newspaper journalist recently indulged: reality TV is dreadful, but then so is reality; I think I'll go away and live in a hut in the jungle, except that they're already doing that in reality TV; no, irony is all that is left. And the reader has only to concur: yes, how intelligent, how true! These despairing values, cloaked in gallows humour, are none the less fairly typical of the media and of many highly educated and intelligent people who have opted to live as commentators and chatterers rather than commit themselves to facing the personal, social and cultural problems around them. Is this not a betrayal of society and of the whole human world? Can we ignore the people around us, their value as persons, spouses, or friends with their rights and needs, and the unexplored potential of the human intellectual world with the marvels of its creativity, its potential for good, and its capacity for discovery? Beauty, goodness and truth have been understood as the attributes of God for millennia. Why abandon honouring them now, and for what? The values of the postmodern isolate? I doubt that this is what most people truly want.

I start from the view that contemporary secular culture needs to be looked at with fresh eyes. In speaking of culture I am referring to the whole way of life, values and understandings of a community or society, not only its most refined intellectual, scientific, literary or artistic achievements, and it appears to me from my own observation and experience that a sceptical or satirical mentality is choking the life out of our culture. The media make a virtue out of negativity, by claiming to be the voice of rationality, legitimate criticism and cultural freedom. Science exalts itself by claiming autonomy from ethical principles, in the attitude of 'if it can be done then let it be done' in a comic mimicry of the Creator, and many blindly accept science's authority, which becomes a kind of pied piper leading us all we, or they, know not where. And the intellectuals, who should be prophetically warning us through their philosophical and creative works about the swamps we are entering and helping us by plotting our paths to safety, have abandoned their role as guides because they believe in nothing, except perhaps the ephemeral works and texts they produce. They have become false prophets who ignore society's real needs, and lead people further astray through their fruitless ideas and their undermining of the moral and spiritual learning that resides in inherited cultures.

It may be easy to criticise, but what can be said that is truly different? What solutions are there to the uprootedness and confusion of contemporary society? Simply to reiterate the beliefs of an ancient faith is to return to precisely what all these experts have rejected. They had their reasons. It did not satisfy them, personally or intellectually, and they have come to see themselves as living in a 'post-Christian' society. And yet, with the passing of Pope John Paul II, the world witnessed a moment of truth when it could acknowledge not only the greatness but the sanctity of a man who did stand for something different, something that proved its effectiveness in both worldly and spiritual terms.

To explore how such a vision of moral and spiritual commitment can be renewed appeared to me to be the most valuable, because hopeful, contribution I could make with this book. It takes up Pope John Paul's theme of bringing gospel faith to bear on culture, looking for its practical implications, for I am convinced that there are things worth saying that are not sufficiently heard and that do make sense. There will need to be change. People will need to consider living differently. And while many make sensible proposals about protecting the environment or bringing development aid to poor nations, what is lacking in contemporary society is an undergirding philosophy or faith that can not only lead us towards these desirable goals but also motivate us to choose ultimate ends for ourselves, and thus emancipate the young, the intellectuals, and ordinary people too, from confusion and anarchy.

Why should we place any hope in Christian faith, especially if this is a post-Christian age? I believe that a new spiritual awareness is dawning in Western society. We have seen it in the strength of religious belief in the United States, the interest in religion among some of the most intelligent of the young, and in the moral authority exercised by a Pope who outfaced vilification and held tenaciously to transcendent principles and values. It would be a disaster if a way forward existed that continued to be rejected because of old prejudices. The invitation here is to look again at the wisdom and truths of Christian faith: that Jesus Christ is God, that he lived on earth and preached a message that will never pass away, that he accepted death by crucifixion to make a new life possible for all humanity, and that he rose from death into a heavenly glory that he desires all people to share. People who have never seriously considered Christian faith are now doing so, and they might be encouraged to do so even more were it not for the betrayal of the media professionals and the intellectuals who have substituted the froth of postmodern excitement for the grit of the truth, goodness and beauty that could lead people back to their source in God.

What would it mean to *save* secular society? Can we restore faith and hope in the Gospel to secular society and culture? The answer is in one way simple: it is not our responsibility. God can look after his own interests and ensure that his will prevails. However, he has chosen to allow human beings to participate in the work of salvation and spiritual renewal that he assigned directly to Jesus Christ. Pope John Paul II made it a main principle of his pontificate to encourage the Church in this evangelising mission throughout the world, particularly by his Apostolic Exhortations to Europe, America, Africa and Asia, by encouraging the Pontifical Councils for Social Communication and for Culture to undertake critical studies on the media, the Internet, advertising and New Age spirituality, and by returning constantly to the theme of evangelising culture in his speeches and letters.

I shall draw on this work, without which I could not have begun my task, though limiting my canvas particularly to key areas of cultural conflict and change, including the worlds of youth, the media, science and the arts. The work is in two parts, a first part that explores why the Church is called to evangelise and what issues it has to confront, and then a second part that details a practical strategy. I believe that shining the light of Christian faith on intellectual and cultural life can produce fruitful possibilities and conclusions, and show how human culture is awaiting faith and hope in the Kingdom of God already inaugurated by the life, death and resurrection of Jesus Christ. I see a role in this for all people of Christian faith or good will who want to give positive meaning and purpose to their lives. The outcome will in the end depend upon their commitment to an undertaking that has nothing of the ironic or the anarchic, since it involves faith in the divine integrity of truth, goodness and beauty as a genuine option for human beings. It is this faith that will lead them to live with their sights set on higher goals than an agnostic society is able to conceive.

PART ONE
THE CALL TO EVANGELISE

CHAPTER ONE

'Put out into the deep!' (Luke 5:4)

RECENT CONVERSATION ABOUT religion left me rather on the ropes, more because of its intensity than its originality. Some of the points made about 'fundamentalist' Christians and Catholics by one articulate lady were:

- President Bush is supported by fundamentalists who deliberately engage in conflict and want to meet the Muslims head-on. Several American friends had convinced her that she was in an unassailable position. The Iraq war and the torture photos made her think of the Crusades and the Inquisition.

- Christians should be looking for a tolerance whereby they stop trying to convert people and instead show liberal values that have broad appeal. Christianity is losing ground in Europe, and will lose more if it continues to be intolerant.

- The Catholic Church cannot find enough new priests because it has chosen celibacy, which doesn't work because people have sexual urges that they have to do something with, and in the Catholic case it is sex-abuse.
- Muslims and Catholics want to convert the whole world to their way of seeing things, and this is bound to lead to conflict. However, that is the viewpoint of the fundamentalists. There are more accommodating Catholics; and most Muslims do not want conflict but rather peace and coexistence.

Evangelising people and cultures

When Pope John Paul II called for the Church to 'put out into the deep' (NMI, 1 – see list of Church Document Abbreviations, p.259), that is, to go in search of those needing to hear the Gospel preached, he was following closely in the steps of Pope Paul VI who in 1975 framed the challenge: 'The Church exists to evangelise.' (EN, 14) We could therefore say it is the mission of every Christian or Christian community to evangelise. It should be a dimension of everything Christians say about their faith. Yet it seems that the Christ-given mission of preaching of the Gospel to all nations has faltered. In many countries there is a marked loss of faith, a retreat by Christians from leadership in society and culture, and a loss of confidence in the power of the Gospel to change minds and hearts. The phrase 'new evangelisation' was used by Pope John Paul II to call the

Church to what he saw as the unifying mission of the whole Church at the turn of the Millennium (TMA, 21). He sought to stimulate the effort to re-evangelise people who were either once Christian believers themselves or who at least belonged to nations and cultures with a strong Christian core to their values and customs,[1] but who now 'have lost a living sense of the faith, or even no longer consider themselves members of the Church, and live a life far removed from Christ and his Gospel.' (RM, 33)

It is clear that Pope John Paul saw the need for a work of evangelising that met the needs of a generation, even a civilisation that, while it had virtually lost the faith, was none the less seeking spiritual answers. By the end of the age of the apostles the preaching to the nations called for by Jesus was a reality, in the sense of extending to the known world. But now we have the sense that the Gospel has at least to a degree been preached everywhere, that the existence of the print and electronic media has made this feasible at the level of sheer information, and yet it seems that we are returning to the beginning, with so few convinced of the truth of the Good News that the Gospel is becoming a has-been of culture.

Then came the words of Christ repeated by a pope in our time: 'Put out into the deep!' What a powerful summons those words imply. It is not that they did not have exactly the same meaning when Jesus first spoke them, but they could not convey the same challenge in the world of the Roman

Empire as they do now for the Church. The 'new' evangelisation begins from and corresponds to the spiritual concerns of the whole modern and postmodern worlds of culture, belief and morality, with their confusion, rebellions, fears, anxieties and despair. It represents a new direction of thought and the fulfilment of the Church's constant prayer to the Holy Spirit 'to renew the face of the earth'. It can therefore inspire faith and hope, creative human work, and a new spirit of love, unity and peace.

This work has to engage not only with people but with entire cultures that have either never known or otherwise have repudiated the Christian faith. Since the time of the Second Vatican Council the Catholic Church has clearly perceived that human cultures, and indeed many religious traditions in the world, contain 'seeds of the Word' (AG, 11) or 'a ray of that truth that enlightens all' (NA, 2). Moreover, such good things are found sown not only in minds and hearts but also 'in the rites and customs of people' (LG, 17), and therefore Paul VI could assert in *Evangelii Nuntiandi* that the object of evangelisation was not only people but the world they held in common, 'the personal and collective consciousness of people' (EN, 18). The evangelising of culture is constantly happening under the guidance of the Holy Spirit but it has not yet become a fully acknowledged mission for the Church. The main reason the two popes' appeals have not been taken up is the apathy of a Church that has been asleep and divided. It has therefore to be awakened, renewed and purified in such a way as to be able to speak to the hearts of those who feel doubt, suspicion, and even anger or contempt towards the faith. Recent documents of the Church, especially some of the major documents of Pope John Paul and others issued by the Pontifical Councils, have suggested the main guiding principles for the task. It is this rich seam of insights and proposals that I have sought to mine, so as to construct a practical model to guide people of good will in the spiritual renewal of their cultures.

The approach requires, first, that ordinary everyday matters be viewed in a supernatural perspective. I could take the example of the endless and inconclusive discussions by teachers and educationalists about values, a debate which is so uninspiring, and in fact truly uninspired, so long as it neglects God. We evangelise by looking with new eyes at what is going on around us, by looking also for the God's-eye view of our world rather than being blinkered with the empirical and the cultural alone. And so we could pose such questions as 'what about death and thereafter?' or 'why suffer for the sake of an idea, a morality, or another person?' or 'can we speak meaningfully about Jesus in the world today?' or 'is it anything more than piety or quaintness to speak of holiness in modern life?' Partly, this mission is one of finding a language in which to speak about God and virtue in a world which lives in bland indifference. If it can be undertaken successfully it can constitute a wake-up call to faith and an exposure of the false values of secular materialism.

To reveal truth, goodness and beauty in the created world and in divine revelation does not necessarily mean preaching. It rather means becoming aware of these elements in natural and transcendent reality, so that they can become more explicit or more visible to people who had not seen them clearly, or perhaps not at all. Therefore, creative work in literature, the arts, music, science, and the theological arts, becomes the way in which a vision of the truth is shared. Helping others through works of human imagination to see, first the seeds, then the stalks, then the full growth of the ear and the grain of wheat (cf. Mark 4:28), becomes the way that the reality of God is once more revealed to humanity. Creative Christian people, whether writers, artists, musicians, researchers or workers in different occupations and activities, including those that serve in families, schools, hospitals, and communities, use their gifts, insights and imaginations to discern and proclaim the features of God, immanent and transcendent.

Each person living a conscious Christian life is helping to change not just their neighbour's viewpoint, values and beliefs, but the context in which such values are formed and transmitted. Taken in its entirety, this work is the expression through culture of the truth, goodness and beauty that comes ultimately from God, and according to Christian faith, from God absolutely. It is not the promotion of these things in themselves, still less their creation, so much as their discovering, revealing, acknowledging, respecting, cherishing and their echoing in people's lives and work. Since truth, goodness and beauty are the three principal attributes of God, those that encompass and integrate the other attributes, we can say that when we speak of evangelising culture we are not adding or inventing anything. We are but opening our eyes, and helping others to open theirs to what already exists, and we are encouraging the growth of further seeds present in creation so that they can flourish as testimony to the infinite riches of God's creation.

The insight of St Bonaventure that each part of creation reveals the totality is apposite. This is a work of contemplation, but there is a sequence of moving from a feature of creation to the specificity of that work of God, and then to the nature of the Creator whom we praise and adore in all that he has done. This sequence can also be reversed when we recognise God's manifold work and the seeds he has planted in our minds and hearts to enable us to participate in creation and its appreciation, thus giving glory to God. This movement back and forth is the employment of our lives – we too are God's work of art (Eph 2:10). If we fail to realise this we are missing not only the meaning and purposes of life, but the truth, goodness and beauty that can enlighten and save us and all whom we love or for whom we have responsibility as a human family. When the Pontifical Council for Culture published *Towards a Pastoral Approach to Culture*[2] it underlined in general terms this very mission. In an article published in a collection primarily concerned with catechesis I did outline the topic[3], but now I am proposing a more developed approach to what is surely a central and even pivotal idea in the new evangelisation.

The dimension of faith

Both Pope Paul VI and Pope John Paul II were concerned with what they saw as the gap between faith and culture. Evangelisation means seeking to discover what it might mean to close this gap. Some social philosophers have tackled aspects of this problem. For example, Scruton[4] explains very clearly the conflict that has opened up between traditional high culture, that is the culture of the great literature, art and music of the past, and the postmodern character of contemporary culture, but he goes little farther. He acknowledges religious beliefs and values, but does not dwell on the opposition between Christian faith, on the one hand, and culture in its modern, postmodern and essentially secular, indeed secularist forms, on the other. Thus a task presents itself for Christians of sharing the Gospel with those who are unaware of it or who have forgotten its claims on them, but also of outreach to a secular culture so as to evangelise the culture itself. It is this latter idea, one which was new in its expression, though as old as Christianity itself in its reality, that particularly needs clarifying and expanding.

I therefore want to move on several stages, and first to identify secular and postmodern variants of culture, but in relation to the beliefs and values of Christian religion as a distinct culture in itself. Not only is there separation, but there is a cultural struggle, whereby contenders for each worldview, secular or spiritual, are pitted against each other in an apparently irreconcilable conflict. This can be seen in a number of areas of current controversy, but especially in relation to sexual mores and the pro-life/pro-choice debate. There is a need to resolve whether such conflicts are endemic and inevitable aspects of human life, or whether they are issues calling for a definitive resolution for the sake of human welfare and for humanity's eternal salvation. It is clearly a contention of the Gospel that the latter is the case.

If we follow this view, then it is not adequate to tolerate all philosophies and values, to compromise basic principles, or to adopt a relativist morality and an agnostic worldview. Writing not long before he was elected Pope, Benedict XVI characteristically focused upon the crucial nature of Christianity's truth claims:

> *Beyond all particular questions, the real problem lies in the question about truth. Can truth be recognized? Or, is the question about truth simply inappropriate in the realm of religion and belief? But what meaning does belief then have, what positive meaning does religion have, if it cannot be connected with truth?*[5]

This entails the next stage of our task. The essential role of the Church and of every Christian is to proclaim a truth that has been revealed to humanity by God through the life and teachings of Jesus Christ. This means that every human being has the right to know of this truth, but by God's dispensation has also the free will to choose whether or not to assent to it. Therefore, while Christians are not obliged to seek to impose Christian belief on others, they do have a duty to proclaim it to them at least by example, and often by word as well.

Since preaching the Gospel is likely to be most fruitful where the target population is understood in its styles of thought and motivations, study of and insight into individuals' beliefs and values, and the characteristics of the whole cultural environment, are important elements of Christian evangelising. Such a perspective on culture allows us to recognise a context in which faith and belief can be seen to answer questions and fulfil aspirations that are fundamentally and unavoidably characteristic of human existence, even if these responses are mysterious to the human sciences of the day when they offer intimations of another reality that we may call spiritual or transcendental, and which demands not only our attention, but our respect, deference and worship.

It is a work of the Holy Spirit to instil in human minds and hearts the memory and the truth of the gospel precepts and the example shown by Jesus in his earthly life. And it is this example that has to be followed. But what is this way, or how has it happened that we have lost it in our times? In its structure, the book takes it as axiomatic that, again in the words of the greatest missionary after Christ himself: 'they will not hear of him unless they get a preacher, and they will never have a preacher unless one is sent.' (Romans 10:14, Jerusalem Bible version) The Church, in other words, has to recognise its responsibility as perhaps never before, and this means a whole renewal of the Church and the people of God. Indeed, even these will not have heard of Christ, the way, truth and life, unless they get a preacher. In our own day it can certainly be claimed that they have had their preacher in John Paul II, and that they need now to digest his message about putting out into the deep. But it is apparently not as simple as that, because the Church and the people of God themselves need to be evangelised for this call to be meaningful to the greater part of the faithful. It is only then that the mission of Christianity to evangelise the unchurched and the whole of secular culture can be fully understood and carried into effect.

Notes

[1] Ralph Martin and Peter Williamson, eds, *Pope John Paul II and the New Evangelization*. San Francisco: Ignatius Press, 1995; see also RM, 33;VS, 106; NMI, 40.

[2] Pontifical Council for Culture, *Towards a Pastoral Approach to Culture*. PCC,1999.

[3] Dudley Plunkett, 'The New Evangelisation of People and Cultures', in John Redford, ed., *Hear O Islands: Theology and Catechesis in the new Millennium*. Dublin: Veritas, 2002.

[4] Roger Scruton, *An Intelligent Person's Guide to Modern Culture*. London: Duckworth, 1998.

[5] Benedict XVI, *Truth and Tolerance: Christian Belief and World Religions*. Ignatius Press, 2004, Preface.

CHAPTER TWO

Secular Culture and Faith

T HE MAIN PROPOSITION of this chapter is that Christian believers are inevitably involved in a struggle to avoid their faith and way of life being overwhelmed by secular culture. When St Paul says, we should not fight evil with evil, but overcome evil with good, this is not of course a prescription for a kind of pious self-immolation or departure from the field of battle. What it means for Christians today is that they are obliged to wrestle with secular culture in all its forms. We have therefore to identify the sources of the tension between faith and culture, to see how secularism impacts on the beliefs and practice of Christian believers, and from there we can see just what kind of challenge they face. For example, it is the evident intent of many governments around the world to limit the influence of Christian and indeed other religious bodies, or even to force them out of public affairs where they are regarded as having an undue influence or as holding beliefs and values that are at odds with publicly expressed policies or the hidden agendas of powerful social and political forces.

A widely held view is that Christian faith fought a losing battle against the assaults of reason and science which have been deployed especially since the Enlightenment in an effort to prove humanity's autonomy and growing power over nature. In this interpretation it was inevitable that reason would be claimed as invalidating religious faith, that science and technology would be taken as proving humanity's power to meet its own needs without recourse to faith, prayer or divine help, and that it would be expected that religion would become a merely cultural vestige that would eventually die away. In his inspiring book *Christendom Awake*, Aidan Nichols speaks of contemporary culture's rejection of the rational, the moral and the aesthetic in their traditional senses [1]. In many ways these are equivalent to the notions of truth, goodness and beauty. Truth has been rejected by a false idea of science, namely scientism; goodness has been rejected by subjectivism and individualism, and beauty has been rejected by postmodern nihilism. We can extend Nichols' analysis by seeing that the real rebellion is not against any one of these but against their integrity. The critical point is that the reason why secular culture has fallen into these traps is because it has lost the vision of how the three elements interact, sustain and complete each other. They make a coherent unity, like the concept of the balancing effect of the executive, the legislature and the judiciary, or, more aptly, the Trinity itself.

Contemporary values – If one wished to choose a time when the scales appear to have tipped massively in this socio-religious revolution, it might possibly be the 1960s, when a cultural tremor shook the whole human world and set off a secularising movement that affected not only intellectual elites but every stratum of society. With the loss of confidence in a supernaturalist view of reality, there was huge disaffection in the Catholic Church as well as in virtually all other religious bodies and an explosion of morally permissive behaviour no longer seen as subject to traditional norms, especially for example in the sexual area and in the acceptance of liberal views on experimentation in eugenics, embryo research and other hitherto ethically suspect fields. In the decades since the 1960s most of these trends have accelerated, with falling church memberships and attendances, especially in the West, a youth culture that has sought increasing independence from traditional restraints, an increasing moral relativism, and the trend to a globalisation of most of these factors. What is perhaps most striking, at least in its strength of expression in Western democracies, is an antagonism towards organised religion that can be discerned not only in secular movements but also in governments and international organisations.

By the closing years of the twentieth century it became possible to characterise these trends in a new way. In matters of moral life, in social and economic decisions, and in religious or spiritual seeking, the principle of personal choice came to be accorded an overwhelming importance. Individualism was not new, but the emphasis on choice which transformed Western culture and its debates about abortion, human rights, women's issues, and church decision-making was breathtaking in its impact. In the world of literature, the arts and the media this same process had been characterised as the advent of postmodernity. This was understood as the consequence of a widespread collapse of confidence in rationality, with many creative minds of high culture and even spirituality committed to deconstructing all forms of authority and substituting the *authority* of the individual consciousness. All perspectives were to be respected because none was entitled to claim precedence.

This outlook has been said to be nihilistic, because in claiming that everyone is entitled to their view of reality such thinkers undermine any collective understanding and thus notionally abolish the legitimacy of society, institutions and government at one fell swoop. Paradoxically, of course, it is part of this new consciousness that everyone should accept its conclusions, and thus we have the phenomena of political correctness, a new cultural totalitarianism, and special rules that empower such pressure groups as radical feminists, gay liberationists and various minority interests to command attention to their claims and to shame all those who do not conform.

Reason, self-interest and postmodern cultural values drive people away from faith in God, while faith invites a constant attention to, and a learning from God. The decision to exclude religious faith from culture follows the conviction that humanity is independent of any notion of God. Religious faith is perceived either as rigid and irrational, or as following a political agenda. The revolt against traditional beliefs is shown in the public taste for satire and in the loss of moral sense in matters of honesty and sexual morality. Moral relativism and a postmodern eclipse of rationality combine to focus upon the rights of the individual or the self as a self-evident value and object of esteem, if not of worship.

The illusion of autonomy – It becomes virtually impossible to invoke God's name or his will in a culture that is inflated with its own knowledge, technology and self-will. People choose to impose their own meaning on life, which is either an ideology to which they have become conditioned, a fashion that has become dominant in society, or a desire for self-aggrandisement. Why is it that people find themselves unable to acknowledge certain things that are staring them in the face: the racial suicide of abortion, the degeneration of sexual licence from free love to child sex abuse and other perversions, the corruption of material excess, the hopelessness of drink and drug addiction, the brutalising effect of eugenics and euthanasia, the false logic by which the privileges of the rich societies and neglect of the poor are justified, and the evasions, injustices and self-destructions resulting from warlike feelings in self and society?

The notion of a meaning and purpose for life linking humanity to its Creator has become something inaccessible, in fact meaningless to many contemporaries. It is not that all such people are atheists, but they have become indifferent, and live as though there was no God. Believers are nearly silent in front of what Pope John Paul called the generalised apostasy that is taking place in contemporary Europe. A similar process is occurring in North America, in Canada even more than the United States, whereby the name and influence of God is being rejected by law and by changing mores. The most dramatic example of this process is in the area of family, with current social and legal redefinitions allowing for the creation of alternatives to the traditional family of mother, father and children. This is only the conclusion of a long process of progressive breakdown of the family assisted by law, through divorce, the abrogation of laws against sexual depravity, putative rights of children against their parents, and so forth. These legal changes are supported by a shift in social attitudes to sexuality and by feminist challenges to males and to fatherhood. Moral failure in the traditional family and the rebellion against faith and the values it sustained have led to a diminished awareness of doctrine among Christian believers and a fall in the religious practice of sacramental marriage.

What this amounts to for secular society is the loosening, if not the breaking up of its moorings to the world of the spirit and of faith, and therefore a widespread existential self-questioning or, perhaps more often, a bland refusal to consider the serious questions of life. In a major summary of Catholic social teaching, the Pontifical Council for Justice and Peace puts it:

Without a metaphysical perspective, the loss of a longing for God in self-serving narcissism and the varied means found in a consumeristic lifestyle, the primacy given to technology and scientific research as ends in themselves, the emphasis placed on appearance ...: all of these phenomena must be understood in their cultural aspects and placed in relation to the central issues of the human person..., and of the constant human search for an answer to the great questions that run throughout life.[2]

In commenting on Pope John Paul's Encyclical *Fides et Ratio*, Pope Benedict showed himself sensitive to this very thought, and appreciative of his predecessor for what he was pointing out to modern humanity about its need to continue its metaphysical search:

...if we no longer speak about God and man, about sin and grace, about death and eternal life, then all that remains is sound and fury, a useless attempt to cover up the silencing of what is authentically human. With the fearless frankness of faith, the Pope has pitted himself against the danger of this silence and in doing so he has rendered a service not only to the Church, but to humanity as well.[3]

The marginalisation of religion

A French sociologist has suggested that contemporary society exculturates religion, faith, the Church, religious belief and language.[4] That is, society totally marginalises and ignores, or completely misunderstands or misrepresents religion. Religion is taken out of the mainstream. What used to be the way of life of the people comes to be regarded as out of date, superstitious, ignorant, unsophisticated, illusory, and superseded by secular rationalism, science, empirical evidence, or a new capacity to see through tricks played on earlier generations by interested parties, elites, or the clergy. The taken for granted world of religious faith is seen as discredited, and aspects of daily life thought important by generations of church-going people have been set aside and dismissed from serious consideration. What remains for the secular mind is the conviction of achieving a purified view of social reality.

The whole religious sphere of experience becomes almost impossible to communicate without embarrassment felt by the speaker, and disapproval or contempt by the listener. In these circumstances it seems that many Christians are ashamed of the Gospel. It seems undeniable at least that they do moderate their thoughts and behaviour when dealing with people of a secularist mind-set. The evidence for this exculturation is all around us, especially in the failure of the Press or other media to give religion fair analysis and due attention. There is a creeping change of morals going on that scarcely receives comment. A prominent journalist could say with impunity that Pope John Paul was a political disaster, that he perpetrated a crime against Africa with his teaching on contraception. No one is supposed to dissent from this view, even though a few decades previously the sexual promiscuity that underlies the Aids crisis would have been inconceivable and any manifestations of it universally condemned.

This is not to say that there is necessarily an organised conspiracy against religion but that there is a tendency of contemporary culture to discount faith and its claims. An individual would not be able to effect this. He would not have the influence or sufficient knowledge. But the synergy of media personnel, politicians and legislators, scientific and medical experts, academics in the humanities, and even death-of-God theologians or clergy who are seeking to bring the churches into line with the modern world, all have the effect of removing from the churches their claim to be taken seriously for what they have traditionally represented. Even the culture of the Church, its way of life, its customs and festivals, its forms of speech, its morality and ideals, or its beliefs, are all disempowered by the approved scepticism, the politically correct viewpoint that has street credibility and consensual approval in modern conversation. The process is subtle but devastatingly effective. To question it is to court condemnation or ridicule, yet to counter or reverse this dominant secularism is precisely the challenge for Christians today.

It is obvious that many of these exculturating trends over recent decades were strengthened by the fact that they were not clearly perceived, or certainly not challenged by religious believers through family life, education, use of the mass media, or even Church teaching on any level but that of the Magisterium. By contrast, many liberal-minded theologians have condoned values of contemporary culture, and have thus assisted the secularising process, in spite of the fact that their rational tenets have become increasingly untenable within a postmodern culture. That is, progressive theologians who responded to the notion that contemporary worldviews needed to be founded upon rationality and should make common cause with secular values, have in fact disqualified themselves from offering what society most needs: a recognition of the holistic and the holy in giving meaning and purpose to anything other than individual or narrow corporate interests. Such theologians thus became irrelevant to people's deepest existential concerns.[5]

Undoubtedly civil society is experiencing a crisis of values at the present time, and many of the undertakings of modern society, in areas such as science, medicine, politics and economics, are in jeopardy because we cannot reach agreement about the direction we want to go, or about reasons for following one way rather than another. Obvious examples would be those in the ethical field concerning such matters as embryo research, cloning, or fertility treatment. However banal it may seem to speak of major social changes since 1945, have they not been such as to alter the basis for social cohesion and moral conviction? On almost any indicator of attitudes, beliefs and behaviour people have changed radically throughout the world in their religious orthodoxy and practice, in the credit attached to established social institutions, in attachment to the structure of the traditional family, in strength of local community feeling, and in rates of criminality of all kinds. On the other hand, it cannot be denied that people have generally become more internationally-minded, more accepting of different races, more sympathetic to the cause of women's rights, more tolerant of variations in lifestyle and sexual mores, and that there is a level of generosity in responding to world needs and catastrophes that is something new and substantial.

Looking at the whole situation from a different perspective, we could say that the 'eternal verities' have been almost totally marginalised because of the widening gulf between faith and culture, or between those who espouse a religious faith and those who reject it. The notion of absolute values, of truth, goodness, communion, or hope, reflecting the existence of a divine presence and an unalterable promise conveyed to us through Scripture, no longer commands general credence. From a Christian view, therefore, there is an extraordinarily acute crisis, one touching the very survival of Christianity, or one which pits the essence of belief in the Gospel against the radically relativist character of contemporary society. This is the reason why it seems of central importance in this book to make a strong critique of secular values which precisely work against gospel values because, with their claims either to rationality or to individual rights, they are in the end value-neutral, non-values, or anti-values posing as values. This is the values crisis, one that is recognisable when viewed from the viewpoint of religious belief, even if it is invisible to many who adopt a secular analysis. Indeed, for Christians and others of religious beliefs, the limits of both rationalism and secularism lie in the taboo that they have applied to the consideration of spiritual values and understandings of human life.

The need for renewal of the Church

If this analysis seems partial or even prejudiced it is a measure of how far the crisis has advanced. If faith and culture have grown apart either because of human error, personal sinfulness, lack of understanding and balance, or through the influence of spiritual powers seeking to thwart

God's plan of salvation, then it forms part of the duty of Christians to seek to build anew a dynamic relationship between them, one through which each is allowed to develop and thrive. Why then is the clear challenge to undertake a 'new evangelisation' not being met more energetically in the Church? The work of spreading the Gospel in Western societies is seen to have faltered to such an extent that even self-confessing Christians are caught in a paralysis. The work has been left to the sterling few who have remained faithful: Pope John Paul, certain bishops and Church leaders, some key figures in religious life and new ecclesial communities, and others who have striven to be true apostles, or who make information about the faith available through the Christian Press, other mass media and the Internet. Yet, if the Church exists to evangelise, it should be every person, every day, every opportunity, and with the grace of God.

But the fact is that the Catholic Church is losing adherents in those parts of the world in which it most flourished in past times. I want then to look at the evidence that the Church is failing to recognise many aspects of its own culture and social environment, including the Christian environment, which constitute a block to its mission to share the good news of salvation. It is not a matter of accusing Christians individually of omissions, but rather of seeing the state of whole sections of the Church worldwide today, divided, rebellious, uncertain, unfaithful, and also mocked for its failure to practise what it preaches. Pope John Paul called for the renewal of the Church, and for the response of every Christian who is awake or can be awakened, to play their part in the co-redeeming venture that Jesus instigated and is still leading. It is in this sense that the Pope called the Catholic Church to the new evangelisation. It is still the same mission to which Christ originally summoned the apostles, but it is new in its setting and approach. Better then to say that the whole apostolate is to be 'renewed', and there is not a single Christian of any denomination who can gainsay this.

A real spiritual vitality characterises many Protestant churches that maintain strong communities, have a tradition of service, and believe in prayer and worship, even if they are not motivated to look sympathetically towards the Catholic Church. But how much do Catholics appreciate the house churches, the strong service orientation, the concern with families, the young, the old, the sick, and the confidence in intercessory prayer, prayer ministry, prayer for healing and the gifts of the Spirit that are often in evidence in Protestant charismatic communities? Is there not a real neglect in the Catholic Church in the West of this new life that God is offering through the presence and activity of the Holy Spirit (TMA, 45) and the charisms and collaborative efforts of the new ecclesial communities and other initiatives in the new evangelisation? If this is so, how can this neglect be explained?

There is a degree of lethargy and complacency in the Catholic Church, especially in Western Europe, and a lack of love, generosity, self-discipline, energy, integrity, courage, hope, and perhaps even faith - though Catholics may often think that they believe! How different in practice, though, are such believers from non-believers who are lazy about seeking meaning for their existences, who are indifferent to religion, who put holy things out of their minds rather than even thinking about them, or who are insensitive to the divine and the spiritual? Perhaps the position of such Christians is morally worse, since believers should know that God never obliges, he only proposes. He may be offering opportunities for conversion and evangelising that are not being noticed, or which are being disregarded by believers who prefer not to be disturbed or challenged. There is little direct teaching from the clergy, or passing on of the teaching of recent Church documents on this topic. Few people are trained to be able to present the faith effectively to non-believers through witnessing, catechesis or apologetics. There is often suspicion among priests and laity alike of what is seen as theological novelty from members of prayer groups, Alpha groups, new movements or charismatic groups when they plead for a greater openness to the Holy Spirit or for evangelising initiatives, and this despite the enthusiastic endorsement of their efforts by Pope John Paul.

Privatised religion - The Church in Europe is inward-looking, and religion is privatised. There are routines for its organisation, its liturgy and prayers, and its sacraments, but the ingredient of outreach seems defective. Despite its strong devotion, worship, and special reverence for the Eucharist, the Church seems tired and cowed by the secular world and to have lost confidence in the promises of the Gospel. The high average age of clergy in Europe is contributing to this exhaustion and inability to cope with challenges, with many parish clergy resistant to both organisational change and spiritual renewal. Even the bishops may be failing to understand what is at stake. The evangelising of the bishops is a mission that American Catholic lay people, and even those of orthodox persuasion, seem to have assumed,[6] while in Europe, clerical/lay divisions lead to discouragement of creativity, marginalisation of initiatives, and a widespread attitude of leaving everything to the clergy. While more is heard about the excluding of women from positions of power in the Church, the real loser is often the lay man whose offer of leadership more obviously rivals that of the clergy.

The privatisation of European Christian faith has untold repercussions. It would seem that the vast majority of Christians in Europe at least, but also to a considerable degree in the US, are timid, if not actually frightened to acknowledge their faith publicly. Christianity is culturally persecuted and marginalised to the extent that most do not dare to raise their heads above the parapet of commitment to the point of confidently proclaiming their beliefs. What used to be a prominent feature of European culture, the Christian community living its faith openly and claiming the right to speak on issues and values in the public sphere, has now become nearly invisible. For example, the proposal to include mention of God and Christianity in the European Union Constitution was sustained largely by Pope John Paul, who was not shy about his faith. However, the media, in speaking about the adoption of the Constitution, regularly rehearsed all its aspects except this one. They marginalised it. And the reason they did this was because Christians were unwilling to keep pressing the point. Examples abound of this kind of submission by believers. It has become acceptable for Christians to keep their faith to themselves.

The result is that no one is being obliged to think of the interests of the religious-minded or to take their concerns seriously. Non-believers have come to expect that they will not have to deal with religion. It has become a taboo area. Moreover, few are competent to make any appraisal of religious matters in the media without distortion, such as seeing only a political angle, or viewing the whole topic as an irrelevance in contemporary society. Christians have allowed themselves to be pushed off the edge of the cultural map. They can expect no understanding, still less accommodation, for their concerns, unless they are far more vocal, articulate and challenging. This is to say that the countercultural character and unavoidable relevance of Christian faith to contemporary Europe needs to be reasserted. In Pope John Paul's words:

The evangelisation of culture must show that in today's Europe too it is possible to live the Gospel fully as a path which gives meaning to existence. To this end, pastoral practice must undertake the task of shaping a Christian mentality in ordinary life: in families, in schools, in social communications, in cultural life, in the workplace and the economy, in politics, in leisure-time, in health and in sickness. (EE, 58)

There is no convincing rationale for seeing privatised religion as a positive freedom that allows everyone to have their own personal beliefs without troubling others. The Christian faith is meant to trouble others, as Jesus warned: 'I came to bring fire to the earth, and how I wish it were already kindled.' (Luke 12:49) Much of this was clearly stated by Pope John Paul in *Tertio Millennio Adveniente*, where he reminded Christians that they need to examine their consciences on the responsibility they bear for the evils of their time. If they live as though God did not exist, they condone others' religious indifference, ethical confusion and lack of respect for human life. Many Christians, he added, are filled with uncertainty which affects their moral and prayer life, their witness to the truth, and their fidelity and obedience to the Church. (TMA, 36)

The culture of the Church – Christian faith holds it that God has a plan for the world, and that it takes effect, with grace and human cooperation, through the truths of revelation passed on by Scripture, the Church and the work of the Holy Spirit transmitted through tradition, Church teaching and inspiration given to individuals. Faith is, in effect, a culture too. It involves beliefs, values, ways of living, of thinking and reasoning, it is a conveyor of meaning, an arbiter of truth, goodness and beauty, but it is focused upon divine will and authority rather than upon human autonomy. How then can we speak of faith and culture when they are both cultures? Is faith a culture of a different kind? Does it lack something that culture in its more traditional sense contains? My sense of the difference is that faith is revealed; it does not grow by environmental influence but only to be more itself, as in Newman's concept of the development of doctrine. Everything else changes, modifies, is transformed. Faith is simply perfected, as it becomes truer to its origin and its finality in God. The culture of the Church, however, is a wholly different notion from the culture of faith. The Church is a social institution as well as the mystical body of Christ, and therefore it has evolved its own culture that both reflects the zeitgeist and results from its own identity and internal development. This is important to recognise, because it is a mistake to regard everything about the Church as God-given, just as it is a mistake to see the Church purely as a social and political structure.

What then are the social realities that make the Church a culture? It is a worldwide organisation with an historical past which persists in its structures, customs, rules, behaviours and self-understanding. It is also a society governed almost entirely by males, and has a hierarchical organisation dominated by males who are ordained. To be a priest is to have a special place in the Church or, to put it another way, not to be a priest is to lack access to real influence in the Church. Whatever the degree of virtue of a Church official, and at whatever level, there is a convention or presumption that the Church deserves a special respect or moral authority regardless of whether this is seen to be earned in a specific instance. Many aspects of the Church's culture are precisely the type of features that contemporary secular culture questions or rejects even in secular institutions, such as absolute authority and the lack of a democratic structure, the clericalist attitudes of many benefiting from their positions in the Church, the seeking of wisdom by reference more to the past than the present or future, appealing to laws, doctrines and precedent rather than to experience, moral strictures in sexual and other areas, and all non-scientific or unempirical assertions taken as a basis for belief and practice.

Similarly, any lapses in living up to its own code are thrown in the face of the Church as evidence of its hypocrisy, immorality, or irrelevance to many contemporary needs and concerns, and indeed its meaninglessness as a contribution to real life issues. It could perhaps be argued that many such cultural accretions that characterise the Church in the view of its attackers are indeed inimical to its vocation and purposes in the task of the building of God's Kingdom. There is undoubtedly a need for the Church to be more self-critical, not just apologising for its faults but changing, converting, including in secular ways, so that its culture is streamlined to serve contemporary society in a more focused and committed way.

Self-evangelisation of the Church - Pope Paul first called for the self-evangelisation of the Church in *Evangelii Nuntiandi* (EN, 15), and he was echoed in a striking way by Pope John Paul's proposal for an examination of conscience by the Church and a repentance for past failures and injustices (TMA, 34-36). Self-evangelisation certainly includes all that Pope John Paul sought to do in purifying the memory of the Church, expressing sorrow for sins of the past, asking pardon of those wronged, that is, purifying its own culture and removing such barriers to the communication of gospel values as theological conflicts and disunity. However, it is not simply a question of the Church cancelling out wrongdoings, but of its developing a new approach supple enough to relate to its contemporary social environment rather than presenting rigidities to the people and cultures it encounters. The hope and love of the Gospel are needed by today's world: hope to give meaning, love to give purpose to living. However, these can only be offered where they are already practised, and it is this that is an indispensable prerequisite for building bridges to non-Christian, or anti-Christian, cultures. The Church is obliged to strive to apply to its own practice the same stringent principles that it would wish others to assume, as in the media, in educational institutions, or in the field of medical ethics.

Thus, any strategy that has any chance of being effective must begin by purifying the carriers of the message, then of course the gospel message being carried, and finally by ensuring that this message is inculturated in a way that can best be received by those to whom it is being directed. This last aspect involves the specific targeting of the message for the particular culture, to cope, for example, with its human problems, its rationalism, its moral relativism, false spiritualism or nihilistic values. While this huge task is primarily a spiritual one, it is also a theological and broadly intellectual undertaking, since it demands psychological and sociological understanding and a creative pedagogy across the whole culture, including its institutions, laws, social customs and values. It is this fruitful combination of spiritual, theological and social-scientific insights that empowers the evangelising Church to offer a genuinely prophetic message. The character of this self-evangelisation will become clearer as the argument of the book advances, and I return to the topic specifically in Chapter 8.

NOTES

[1] Aidan Nichols OP, *Christendom Awake: on Re-energising the Church in Culture*. Edinburgh: T&T Clark, 1999.

[2] Pontifical Council for Justice and Peace, *Compendium of the Social Doctrine of the Church*. Libreria Editrice Vaticana, 2004, para. 554.

[3] Benedict XVI, 'Culture and Truth: Some Reflections on the Encyclical Letter Fides et Ratio', a lecture at, St Patrick Seminary, Menlo Park, 13 February 1999.

[4] Danièle Hervieu-Léger, *Catholicisme, la fin d'un monde*. Paris: Bayard, 2003.

[5] Harvey Cox, *The Secular City,* Harmondsworth: Penguin, 1968, refers to the notion of 'religionless Christianity', a faith that has become totally absorbed into the culture.

[6] Russell Shaw, 'An open letter to America's bishops', *Crisis Magazine*, June 2004.

CHAPTER THREE

Evangelising Secular Culture

N ENTRUSTING TO the apostles the task of preaching the Gospel to all nations (Matthew 28) Jesus clearly did not mean to restrict evangelising to individuals. This can be seen from the way he constantly refers to the collectivity of Israel or the House of Jacob. Nations comprise not only individuals but cultures and their peoples' ways of living and reflecting upon their existences. So when we speak of evangelising cultures we envisage all the ways in which the influence of Christian truths and values is brought to bear upon a people's way of life. When certain contemporary cultures on the Western model are seeking to marginalise faith and religion as independent forces in society in order to erect the ideal of a purely secular society with no traces of God, Christians are correspondingly obliged to revive the truths and values of the Gospel through their ways of living, laws and institutions, art, use of technology, medicine, and media, so that God's Kingdom may be restored.

From the Christian viewpoint, faith is a kind of knowledge that is non-empirical, and yet certain. It is also partially experiential, since we can come to a greater faith through experience. Thus, we find that faith is supported by what we come to know of life in the living of it, as regards persons, the value of sacrifice, our sense of the spiritual, the answering of prayer, and so many other things which, taken alone, might carry little conviction. In practice such elements reinforce one another over a lifetime until they are granted credence. Faith can be threatened, and sometimes disappears, and the dark night of the soul may at times seem to obscure the precious truth. Yet part of the faith is to know that it is granted to us to decide for faith, that our will is required to play a part, to give its assent, for without this personal commitment we would be mere puppets with someone else deciding everything for us.

Every effort made by people to assist contemporary society to make a place for the faith in its culture, to recognise the dimensions of truth, goodness and beauty which enlighten, liberate and sanctify, is itself to evangelise culture. We could cite the lives and actions of the saints, the career of a John Paul II, the spiritual journey of St Thomas More or the recent Polish martyrs, Fr Jerzy Popieluszko and Maximilian Kolbe. Equally, Christian education and catechesis, as well as all intellectual work motivated by the

Gospel, are contributions to the reconciliation of faith and culture. However, the project goes beyond this, since it is for Christians to contribute to the development of culture through original intellectual work, the development of just laws and government, works of discovery and invention, creative works, new forms of spiritual engagement, social solidarity, and myriad other ways in which the vision of humanity can be extended to encompass more of God's creation and plan. There will be more to say on this topic in Chapter 9.

These thoughts favour a new approach in the sociology of knowledge and culture in which values, beliefs and faith find a meaningful place. Going further, I suggest there is culturology of faith that has always given results but which has somehow come to be ignored. Modern psychology has studied the traumatic and the dysfunctional, but has missed the ordinary everyday realities of virtue, fidelity, holiness, and all the attributes of spirituality. It is not that no one has had these features of society in mind, since the Church has laboured to encourage them, but they have not been noticed in such a way as to enable us to set them against the fruits of secularism, and thus to raise the issue of how incomplete contemporary society's notion of culture has been.

In fact it becomes evident that there was an evasion of reality, either through incomprehension, ignorance or guile, that meant that certain questions about happiness, holiness, or the supernatural were not, or could not, be asked, and thus that potentially vital aspects of human experience were systematically excluded from analysis or even consideration. Once we dismiss this mind-set it becomes possible to look at such realities as prayer, faith, trust in God, goodness, beauty and truth as accepted features of a total environment, features which explain values and actions and which bring actual answers and real satisfactions. From this it is a short step to begin conceiving strategies to transcend poorer concepts of culture, such as the secular or the postmodern, so as to embrace the dimensions of faith and the spirit. In other words, the evangelisation of culture is a way of seeking divine wisdom and blessings for our world.

A pastoral approach

John Paul II's call to bring gospel values to bear in society and culture has been frequently echoed in contemporary Church documents, for example in the Pontifical Council for Culture's *Towards a Pastoral Approach to Culture*, but the discussion is largely at an abstract level. The 'Towards' of TPAC's title reveals the uncertainties of the first steps being taken in this field. The notion of a pastoral approach is so diffuse that it is difficult to apply in practice, especially as we are dealing with unfamiliar ideas and with little clarity about method. However, culture is constantly being evangelised, and we can learn a great deal simply from reflecting on how this is happening and from there seeking to project forwards to how this pivotal pastoral strategy can be fostered. Recent

Church teaching has repeatedly stressed the guiding principles. In *Evangelii Nuntiandi*, Pope Paul said:

> *The split between the Gospel and culture is without a*
> *doubt the drama of our time, just as it was of other times.*
> *therefore every effort must be made to ensure a full*
> *evangelisation of culture, or more correctly of cultures.*
> *They have to be regenerated by an encounter with the*
> *Gospel. But this encounter will not take place if the*
> *Gospel is not proclaimed.* (EN, 20)

This perspective has featured in Church documents ever since. Pope John Paul said:

> *... the Gospel penetrates the very life of cultures, becomes*
> *incarnate in them, overcoming those cultural elements*
> *that are incompatible with the faith and Christian living*
> *and raising their values to the mystery of salvation which*
> *comes from Christ. (Pastores dabo vobis, 55)*

This is an awesome idea that I believe has not yet received sufficient recognition and understanding. If a whole culture has developed around atheism, materialism, consumerism, moral relativism and a rejection of the value of life and the civilisation of love, an individual has little chance of detaching himself from it without a massive re-education. It will be necessary to confront secular culture as a way of life and understanding that contradicts the Gospel and then to offer a countercultural witness to revealed truth and Church teachings, while searching out in culture those elements, values, customs and achievements that are common to Christian faith, and which can provide ways of access to fuller awareness of, and belief in, its truths. Just like people, cultures are dynamic. They are growing, searching and experimenting. And therefore they need direction and guidance. To evangelise a culture is to enable it to become open to the Holy Spirit and to the truth of the Gospel.

TPAC indicates what is needed as 'revitalising a de-christianised world whose only Christian references are of a cultural nature' (TPAC, 1). The Gospel is a sign of contradiction for a world without God, but the way in which that Gospel needs to be proclaimed must include all the media of social communication both as instrument and object of evangelisation, from family life and schooling to liturgy, academia, the arts, science, politics and social welfare, or every facet of modern life taken not only singly but together as a system of values and mores, that is, a culture.

This Good News addresses human persons in their complex wholeness, spiritual and moral, economic and political, cultural and social. The Church therefore does not hesitate to speak of the evangelization of cultures, that is to say mentalities, customs and behaviour. (TPAC, 4)

The pastoral approach proposed by TPAC was the beginning of a reflection upon a method for evangelising culture. In that regard it was inspirational, and in fact invited more focused work. Many sectors of human life are addressed schematically in the 'Concrete Proposals' section of TPAC, leaving room for further development, but others are conspicuously absent. Where, for example, in this perspective, do we situate New Age beliefs, political correctness, radical feminism, and other aspects of postmodern culture that are at best fleetingly reflected in the document?

It is not surprising that there should be a gulf between the broad principles for evangelising contained in strategic documents from Vatican bodies and the specific actions of often highly pragmatic evangelising agencies and communities, but this gap needs to be filled by thoughtful analysis and planning to outline a whole methodology for evangelising culture. Perhaps the example of liberation theology in Latin America illustrates this need most graphically. A false diagnosis, which placed social and political needs before spiritual and human ones, ensured that many people were lost by the Catholic Church to Evangelical and Pentecostal groups who understood better the felt needs of the poor for basic living resources, care, spirituality and healing.[1] The early generation of liberation theologians could not evangelise the culture of the people, however much they sought to do so through base communities and group meditation on the Word of God, because they were caught up in an agenda that did not itself come from the Gospel of the Beatitudes.

And while we complain about adverse portrayals of faith by the media, should we not also ask if the promoting of Christian ideas and values is not itself a work of evangelising culture as well as being a protest against the falseness of relativism and secularisation? For this it would seem that we need a new apologetics, a new language for speaking about spiritual values and religious truths, and a closer attention to the religious richness of metaphor and image, beauty and virtue, and of everything that can speak to us of God and his revelation in the created world and our own consciousnesses. Part of this seeking for a language is seeking alternatives to words, that is, actions that are of the Gospel, actions that reflect values that are timeless, that relate to absolutes. But there is also the possibility of finding a language of the arts, or of a person-centred philosophy, that can speak to modern society. Christians cannot give up on the possibility of being heard in words as well as actions. They may need to refresh the topics that they address, and instead of using traditional terms such as dogma, morality, ritual or piety, they have to substitute rights, fairness, culture, loyalty, friendship, wonder, beauty, that is, a language that is filled with positive values but reflects contemporary struggles as much as traditional solutions. Putting it another way, there has been a new Reformation in the spread of modernism and postmodernism even within the Christian Church. Now we are witnessing a new counter-Reformation, a reclaiming of the ground lost, a new proclamation of the Gospel where it had been forgotten or abandoned.

I personally recall that, at exactly the same time that I was reading Hervieu-Léger's analysis of the 'exculturation' of the faith in Paris, I also noticed an impressive number of new books on religious themes. I visited an exhibition of the work of Marc Chagall filled with intriguing religious imagery. I saw a collection of Christian icons of the Arab world, and I encountered crowds of worshippers and sightseers in the churches of the Rue du Bac, Notre Dame and Sacré Coeur. We need to remind ourselves that while some see exculturation we must reject any deliberate self-blinding or the refusal to face an obvious fact of history and experience: the continuing vitality of Christian belief, thought and art.

A seven-step strategy

What, then, is the work to be done? It is truly vast. However the first steps are clear. Christians have to make a commitment of will to respond to the promptings of the Spirit to emerge from ghettoes, to see what is happening in the secular world, to enter into spiritual activities and social communications that are being neglected, to explore, study and exploit new opportunities for dialogue, proclamation and discipling. Evangelising culture is part of this initiative, in which the objective is less to attain individual conversions than to remove barriers, encourage seeking, offer love, instil hope, and make faith a possible option for a generation without God. It is an exciting challenge, for it consists in nothing less than a re-evaluation of the role of the Church in the modern world, consistent with *Gaudium et Spes*, the great statement on contemporary society by the Second Vatican Council, but re-envisioned for a secular and postmodern culture, and understood as a work of the Spirit. Indeed, nothing less than a new Pentecost is needed in a civilisation that has become decadent and self-destructive while convinced of its superiority over all preceding cultures.

How is this to be done, and what is the responsibility of the Christian believer? Would it make any sense to say that this task is to be undertaken by the Church or any specific agencies of the Church without it being the responsibility of every Christian? Indeed, as a parent, a citizen, a television viewer, a worker in the economy, artist, writer, football fan or churchgoer, the Christian forms part of both the faith community and the culture. It is in his or her living experience that the link between faith and culture must first be made before it can be established more generally in society. This is why we can say that it is Christians' business today to understand and respond to the crisis of the gulf between faith and culture.

I have envisaged the evangelising of culture as an approach or strategy consisting of seven steps. These are set out as a progression from developing awareness of the issues to taking action that is both practical and spiritual in nature.

Step 1. Developing a dialogue – engaging with secular culture to observe and analyse elements of cultures, comparing the values they reflect to those of the Gospel and discerning those positive elements that contain seeds of the Gospel.

Step 2. Exposing moral relativism – actively identifying discrepancies between faith and culture in fundamental values and assumptions, so that Christians can expose them and address them with respect and empathy, correcting moral errors and illusions with information and rational argument, especially purifying those aspects of contemporary culture that demean or ridicule the religious worldview.

Step 3. Witnessing to the Gospel – in what it proposes not only regarding particular issues but as a coherent message of truths and ways of life. Christians recognise such messages as revealed by God in creation. They see the Maker in the things he has made and they are therefore able to find the transcendent in the everyday.

Step 4. Awakening faith - by evangelising people to bring them to gospel beliefs and ways of life through conversion or renewal of faith. In evangelising cultures, on the other hand, a whole spiritual revolution is being promoted, and conversion is encouraged not only as personal decisions but as cultural movements.

Step 5. Teaching and inspiring Christian faith and life –
seeing these as major ongoing responsibilities of the Church.
By its influence on families and schools the Church has
spread Christian faith and life. Catholic schools aim to
educate and form people so that they appreciate and
assimilate the fulness of Christian doctrine. Christian
teachers and catechists respond to people's spiritual needs,
and help them to open themselves to the transcendent.

Step 6. Creating beauty - this is God's work, but he invites
human collaboration. If we intend to explore practically
what it means to bring gospel values to bear in society and
culture, this opens up a huge potential for apostolic action.
By seeking out, revealing and finding ways to express God's
truth, goodness and beauty, all human beings can participate
in his creative work.

Step 7. Renewing the face of the earth - this is the work
of the Holy Spirit, but the evangelist's thrust is crucial since
it pleases God to work through human instruments however
weak or undeserving. Truth, goodness and beauty are of
God's Kingdom and we can only truly know and express
them through his revelation and inspiration.

This sequence of steps can, I believe, be discerned from
the New Testament in how Jesus himself preached. In fact the

very words 'New Testament' evoke the unifying factor of his mission, which was to make known to the Jewish people a promise of salvation that built upon and completed the Old Law to which their nation had been subject. In the Sermon on the Mount (Matthew 5-7) we find all the steps needed for the evangelising of culture in our own time. Jesus contrasts the rigorous interpretation of the Mosaic Law or Old Covenant, with its 'eye for an eye', and the merciful love of God which had been obscured by man-made rules (Steps 1 and 2). Gospel values are attested in the Beatitudes of a New Covenant (Step 3). Faith is awakened by the authority he displays (Step 4). The way of prayer and life of the Gospel is inspiringly taught (Step 5). The truth, goodness and beauty of God's providence are described in a luminous passage (Step 6). And the insistence on seeking the Kingdom of God is affirmed as the overall priority for the Christian (Step 7).

While at first sight this may seem a formidable programme, and some may think that this is not their direct concern or that the seven steps take them beyond their own capabilities, I want to argue that it is all part of our concern, whoever we are - I would even say Christian or not. The reason is that this is not a plan to manipulate people or to conquer the world for Christianity by stealth. It is about finding the best way for human beings to live on the planet together, while leaving open to those who have faith the option of preparing themselves for life after death. If you think you can only manage the first step, and perhaps partially the second, I would say: no, you can go all the way. This is not a job for experts, and certainly not for the public figures, let alone politicians who usually monopolise getting things done on this earth. This is a task for the good - in Christian terms, for saints. The world needs more good people, more saints in fact. They will be the ones who will change everything for the better. And of course the believer asserts that this is not because of their inherent qualities but because they more fully reflect the qualities of Almighty God.

So the appeal to the reader is to pursue the description and the illustration of the seven-step approach in the following chapters, and to recognise that there is a way in which any committed person can contribute to its realisation, just by being what it is given to them to be, whether parent, teacher, priest, or even politician, and through their everyday activity, conversation, work and prayers. The purpose of the book is to encourage people of good will to pursue the project of transforming culture so that it more fully expresses the qualities of truth, goodness and beauty that believers find first and foremost in God. If I use the metaphor of *wrestling* to describe what is asked of the Christian, it is less in the sense of a polemical debate or a struggle against human enemies than an encounter with 'the spiritual forces of evil' (Eph 6:12).

NOTES

[1] Ralph Martin, *The Catholic Church at the End of an Age*. San Francisco: Ignatius Press, 1994.

PART TWO
WRESTLING WITH CULTURE: THE SEVEN STEPS

CHAPTER FOUR

Developing a Dialogue

SECULAR CULTURE VIEWS faith across a chasm of antagonisms, rivalries or indifference, a gap difficult for faith to bridge because of the lack of a common language or commonly acknowledged points of entry or concerns. Faith is viewed with suspicion in contemporary culture when there is any hint of an evangelising purpose, since all claims to authority are seen as fundamentalist, sectarian, arrogant or else evidence of a person's suffering from a psychological condition or need of a crutch for their own life. Faith is seen as invalidated by science rather than as an essential complement to it, or another way of knowing. Specific faith events or tenets, such as the Virgin birth, the resurrection, Eucharistic consecration, the value of prayer or the possibility of miracles, are all seen as human inventions. Mystical experiences, messages from God, divine interventions, signs and similar phenomena are often excluded without any consideration of evidence, and the individuals reporting such experiences are perceived as misguided or corrupt. What place is there in a secular world for understanding the authenticity of such occurrences as Church renewal, new movements or pro-life initiatives as mature developments in spiritual insight? And yet this is exactly the problem faced by St Paul when he arrived in Athens hoping to preach the resurrection in a pagan city. Paul's response to this challenge (Acts 17:16-34) provides a neat encapsulation of the approach I am proposing in this book. H e begins by intriguing the Athenians who enjoy discussion of the latest ideas.

Step one
developing a dialogue with non-believers

What this means for Christians is that there is a need for ongoing efforts to engage with what is happening in the wider society. While negative elements cannot always be directly countered, for example through intellectual repudiation or through legislation, the word can always be spoken, the witness given, or the insight offered, and thus often a dialogue initiated. Even where there is a strong reluctance to respond on the part of secular culture it is the quality of never being discouraged that has always marked the Christian evangelist. So many stories of conversion include an incident where a person receives insight into the faith as the result of finally hearing a word that has been repeatedly spoken, or the sudden memory of a word spoken in the past. Evangelisation cannot be a one-way process. It involves an encounter between persons. Difficulties of communication can only be resolved by cooperation and mutual love. The qualities needed are love, trust and courage, but these have to be experienced reciprocally if there is to be any real fruit. Which evangeliser does not find repentance, humility, love and purification in a genuine evangelising encounter?

It is unfortunate that dialogue over current controversial issues, such as world population control, life issues, suffering, or meaning and purpose for life, is often dismissed on the secular side as dealing with bigotry. Even the desire to share with others the wonders of God's creation cannot be accepted because the notion that such phenomena are created is not regarded as imaginable. Mainstream culture, in seeking to declare its autonomy with respect to the Creator, has foresworn its true goal.[1] We can see this unilateral declaration of independence in several spheres. Upholding reason as humanity's most distinguished faculty, many scientists and intellectuals have decided that there is no God above reason.

In the realm of science this has led to the phenomenon of scientism, for whereas in former times science could bow the knee to the Divinity, recognising science itself as his creation or gift to humanity, now many scientists can see no further than their own theories, which of course are continually being falsified or superseded; and therefore in fact there is nothing beyond today's theory. Contemporary science thus provides us with an example of a culture, or perhaps a subculture, within which certain conventions guide us to what can be claimed to be known or proved. Inevitably, however, such knowledge is provisional; it is neither definitive nor absolute. Moreover, it is only because of an unproved assumption of human reason, namely its title to be the only valid way of knowing, that science, or more accurately scientism, asserts its superiority over religion or its denial of any validity to faith.[2] This scientific reductionism is even more pronounced among lay people who, lacking expert knowledge of science, are forced to believe whatever they are told is the professional consensus. Of course, by no means all scientists make this claim, since they see the unfounded basis for it, but then they are obliged to make the separation methodologically between a way of knowing that relies upon empirical evidence, experiment, measurement and reasoning, and a way of knowing that relies upon revelation, personal experience, and the divine gift of faith.

While science is the area that many people continue to imagine is the Achilles' heel of faith, is it not rather the case that faith and reason are best understood as two ways of knowing, each valid in its own sphere and each needing the other for a fuller understanding. As Pope John Paul so persuasively demonstrated in *Fides et Ratio*, we need both faith and reason, the 'two wings on which the human spirit rises to the contemplation of truth.' (FR, 1) Science, using human reason and the evidence and materials of the created world, is able to reveal its properties and powers in a progressively illuminating way, but it can make no sensible comment on why what exists has come to be or whether it has any meaning or purpose. Faith, springing from a gift made to humanity by its Creator, perceives that creation is a work of God intended for his glory, with humanity invited to share that glory by following God's precepts on earth while awaiting union with him in his heavenly Kingdom. The shortcomings of a reductionist science are easily apparent to the believer. Not only is faith defined out of existence but there is no alternative explanation of the mystery of the creation of nature and of humanity in all its complexity and spiritual depth, and ethical issues are progressively excluded. In the Apostolic Exhortation, *Ecclesia in Europa*, Pope John Paul specifically pointed out the insufficiency and inadequacy of scientism in recognising only experimental knowledge as objectively valid, and he proposes instead those ethical criteria which man possesses as inscribed in his very nature. *(EE, 58)*

The initial thrust of this book has been to set the scene for a dialogue between faith and culture leading to a new evangelisation of culture. This is already becoming a growing element of the Church's mission. It appears, for example, in attention given to apologetics, ecumenism, the multicultural and interreligious environment, to theological perspectives on pro-life issues, human rights, youth culture, moral relativism and cultural postmodernism, as well as to Christian and secular understandings of art, media, civic education, and the kinds of ethical and spiritual issues raised by Pope John Paul II in many of his writings and by the Pontifical Councils for Culture and for Social Communication in their documents on culture, communication and new religious movements. These perceive the need for the Church to dialogue with contemporary society by seeking to show the relevance of its faith and doctrine to the joys and sorrows of a secular world that has almost succeeded in stifling belief in a transcendent God and his revealed truth. Christians, however, need to earn the right to such a dialogue by their respect for people of all convictions and none, and by their sincere efforts to understand secular, non-Christian and anti-Christian preoccupations and motivations.

We are therefore naturally led towards a 'pastoral approach'. A pastoral approach certainly does not imply an uncritical or compromising attitude. Perhaps we could not have said this so confidently a few decades ago, but now who will assert that Western science and technology are unmixed blessings for the world? The challenge of the terrorists is precisely that they throw the West's technology back in its face, and the West is without arms to fight a fundamentalist movement, not because it does not have the weapons to kill individuals, but because it does not have the values and truths upon which to base its struggle. It is at least as likely that the West will become converted to Islam as that it will convert Muslims to Western rational materialism. Christian faith is something else. It will not find it possible to make either Western secularism or Islam its bedfellow.

The overcoming of the lethargy and inward-lookingness of the Church is however essential. If Christians were alert to their own threatened situation, if they followed contemporary events and if they learned to make positive use of the media in defending and proclaiming their faith, so much would change. For this to happen in the Catholic Church people would need to give time to studying its faith and teaching, especially in the documents of the Second Vatican Council, the teachings of the popes and bishops, and the *Catechism of the Catholic Church*. They would also need to find new meeting-places with non-believers and make themselves available to others in conversation, in sharing of ideas and by appreciating the needs and concerns of non-believing people. Megaphone diplomacy will not serve in evangelising. Contact is required. While religious groups need to be hospitable to those who approach them, they cannot depend upon this happening. They will need to leave their churches and go in search of non-believers, finding them where they live and on common ground, as in the media, associations, political life, universities, sports facilities and so forth. In this way they would much more fruitfully build on what is positive about contemporary society from a faith standpoint.

Materialistic values in question

The problem with materialism is that it lulls people into a false sense of security, including spiritual security. In a sense this has happened to the whole Western world at the present time. There is a kind of righteousness abroad that legitimises the values of wealth, power and pleasure in such a way as to prevent people from recognising their moral and spiritual needs. Out of huge wealth the West has been able to make small contributions towards the solution of myriad problems in the world, not enough to solve them, but enough to make it easy to spread the delusion that Western society is good, generous, just and compassionate. With this complacency, the West feels free to enjoy its wealth, and so has a carefree attitude to consumption and pleasure, but the freedom of choice it thus worships is in fact confined to a very small proportion of the inhabitants of the world.

An advertising hoarding shows a woman, with plunging neckline of course, who is lovingly holding a bottle of coca cola that has a label inviting entries for a valuable lottery. The caption is: 'Money is the root of all evil? I'll take my chances.' This may be a witty advert, but it is also perverse: it takes the words of St Paul in 1 Timothy, but adds a question mark, the mark of the sceptic. The Pauline text reads in full: 'The love of money is the root of all evils, and there are some who, pursuing it, have wandered away from the faith, and so given their souls any number of fatal wounds.' Ignoring all this, and seizing on the lure of the possible prize money alone, the woman defiantly says: 'I'll take my chances'. Can we not see here the scene of the seductive Eve urging Adam, the public, to eat the forbidden fruit? Is this not the quintessential temptation to seize the worldly over the otherworldly? The viewer is invited to identify with the risk-taker. The stakes in this little image-story are immense. But what is even clearer is that this kind of seduction into wealth and pleasure is endlessly multiplied every day.

Much current TV output fits the description 'bubble-gum of the mind'. It is stultifying. It induces passivity through a predictable diet of domestic scenes, violence and pornography, through which the intellect is put to sleep. Games shows like *The weakest link* or *Who wants to be a millionaire?* use a minimum of imagination and yet can appeal to crude appetites or emotions, far from reason and conscience. Pornography takes this direction much further and depends upon reason and conscience being suppressed by passion or curiosity. The effect of such programming is to corrupt our values, steal our energies, and depress our feelings. Of course, it is easy to understand the appeal of television soaps. They purport to mirror back to people the kinds of lives they lead, or that particular subcultures lead, in a way that satisfies both a desire for realism and a sense of fantasy: 'that could just be me'. If one denies the premise that

that could be me because of some fatal flaw in the genre then it is difficult to feel involved.

One evident flaw is that soaps show little interest in or regard for the spiritual life. Their characters live in an agnostic world. Instead of faith and virtue, what seems to dominate is feelings and the persecution of people who do not meet the common expectations of the culture. This appeals to the lowest common denominator of human interest, but is purposeless, since it can offer no real solutions to any problems posed. This does not stop soaps from seeking to be very up to date by featuring scenarios that are similar to those in current news media, such as unwanted pregnancies, plans for abortions, gay relationships, failed marriages, one-parent families, adulteries and domestic violence. In the same way, the subset of soaps that deal with crime and the law focus on aberrant behaviour and crooked police; even the 'good cops' have to be 'human' in their moral and other failings. The fantasy element comes in through the siting of soaps in attractive locations, through the fiction of enduring neighbourly social structures based almost entirely on blood and personal relationships rather than on social, economic, religious or political institutions, and on the implausible concentration of surprising turns of events that keep the adrenalin flowing. What this amounts to is the demonstration of a fear of the truth, a backing away from the normal and the ordinary, which is a refusal of life, and this in favour of self-indulgent fantasy and submission to the values of the particular subculture portrayed.

The principal objection to the soaps has to do with the harmfulness of their false anthropology and their superficiality that turn everyone into false anthropologists, people acutely informed about certain aspects of human behaviours, but lacking the true anthropologist's understanding of everything in context. Anyone who has this wider view cannot stay interested in these microscopic doings in their emotional limbo. The soaps are a hall of mirrors with true characters just recognisable, but still false in their distortions, that is, their emotionalism, spiritual indifference, microcosmic inwardlookingness, and all the smattering of attributes that are there to hold attention, impress, provide material for imitation, and mesmerise those who lack esteem for themselves and their own lifestyles. Soaps encourage people to look at their own lives as if through a camera. This self- or image-consciousness becomes increasingly common in contemporary social life. Celebrities constantly behave as performers, of course, but they are imitated by ordinary members of the public. Watching televised public events that feature a videotron, the viewer notices that many spectators are at least as concerned to monitor the large screen as to watch the concert, match or whatever; as soon as they appear on the screen their behaviour changes into a performance.

Information rich, wisdom poor – The Internet has made us an information-rich society, but it is becoming steadily clearer that information is not everything. Learning what to do with information, or simply learning what to do, has not become less but rather vastly more important with the communications revolution. The Internet can satisfy our appetite for data, can multiply our perspectives on a given problem, can offer us untold resources for exploration, can keep us up to date on changing situations, and can even provide us with indispensable material relevant to our enquiries, but we can still be at a total loss if we have no criteria for the use of this information, if we have no clear purposes, if we do not understand the vital significance of what we are being shown. In fact the situation we are in can be worsened by the confusion into which we are thrown if we have information-overload. It is easy to reach the point where what seemed a simple choice to be made is now too complex for us to resolve. This is the danger of the Internet. It cannot provide wisdom, discernment or counsel.

We cannot package wisdom the way we package data. We cannot educate people to judge, discern or discriminate the way we can teach them to look things up, collect items of data, or simply swamp themselves in a rush of detail. However, people are left with the illusion that they know more, that they are better off than their forbears, simply because they have this wealth of information. Actually they are worse off if they cannot find their way out of the morass. All they can do is to keep churning it, moving it around, looking at it different ways, presenting it through ingenious displays. This is a problem of our culture, of which the Internet issue is only a symptom. It can only reflect our postmodernism, relativism, pluralism and confusion rather than provide us with objectivity, truth or clarity.

Advertising - Advertising is a very significant aspect of contemporary culture, one from which we can learn a great deal in our Christian reflection, since it is in many ways a mimicry of evangelising. Advertising incorporates values, even though they are often far removed from the values of the Gospel. There is nothing reproachable or immoral in the simple function of advertising to bring to our attention some information that we might not otherwise obtain and that is of potential interest or usefulness to us. However, commercial advertising especially has several features which make it disturbing to the Christian way of life and conscience. It makes profit and materialistic values rather than people's real needs its primary concern, and tempts people to think that they have needs that they did not previously have. Misrepresenting itself to the consumer, it targets the vulnerable, the insecure, the young, or those most easily separated from their money. It creates worries and even illnesses by opening up impossible horizons of materialism, beauty, health, lifestyle and so forth, and it frequently mocks tried and tested ways of living, values and beliefs.

Advertising has revealed to us the power of the practice of mimicking human sexuality as a strategy for control of economic resources. In the commercialisation of sex to market products from cars to holidays, we identify one of the industry's most familiar characteristics. It uses a form of sexual seduction to subject the buyer, who is less aware of what is going on, to the seller, who knows exactly what he is doing. It thus exploits and mistreats, since it destroys the equality of relations between people, and corrupts by using another's very nature against their best interests. Strangely, however, because of the power of our sexuality, the familiarity of the sexual strategies of the market does not make this approach less potent. An already groomed public, which has lost its moral sense and can only see the commercial message regardless of its corrupting nature and injustice, colludes with the degenerate nature of such advertising and is further engulfed and corrupted by it.

It does not stand up as an argument to say that advertising only reflects society, because it is obvious that the huge amounts of money spent to influence behaviour would not be made available if it did not do precisely this. It studies our psychology and persuades us with great skill. But this is only possible because we have the predispositions necessary. We want immediate satisfactions: possessions, luxuries, bodily comforts or food and drink beyond our necessities. It is hard to argue then that advertisers are any more evil than those who are willing to be influenced, since we have to take responsibility for our own actions. Consumer society is a system in which we are all involved. No individual can turn these trends around. We can limit our own consumption, and this is not without symbolic importance; but it cannot solve the problem. Nor can it be said that there is any sustained attack by Christian leaders on consumerism, even though it obviously runs counter to the gospel injunctions of moderation, restraint of vanity, sexuality and wealth, the overcoming of selfishness and the need to think of humanity as a family involving mutual obligations.

Contemporary lifestyles and the spiritual quest

Everyone talks about celebrities: people who are famous for being famous. They are treated by the media with a combination of fascination and contempt. The public offers adulation; the high-minded, unbridled criticism. And yet acres of newsprint and hours of footage chronicle their every movement, action, remark and especially their every misdemeanour. How do we explain this phenomenon? While it has probably always been so, modern media has rendered it omnipresent at least in part because it satisfies a public appetite relatively easily. But the extraordinary concentration on figures of fashion, popular music, film and TV, sport, royalty and aristocracy, theatre and politics, is surely also part of people's search for what is significant, for what can provide clues about the good life, whether there is any model we can follow, and how we can fill our own lives with more meaning by adopting the life of a freer, richer, more creative being about whom we can fantasise and thus partially fulfil ourselves. Something similar happens when we daydream, or when we contemplate mythical figures and heroes of old. And all of this is of course a substitute for religion, in which the lives and deeds of biblical figures, the stories of the New Testament and the virtues of the saints, were the staple of public imagination for millennia before mass media existed.

I do not think it can be considered fanciful to see the extreme adulation of pop stars as a kind of worship for those who have nothing else to worship. While not implying that there is a conscious spiritual motive at work, I think that the urge to associate, even in the imagination, with the very rich, famous, or glamorous is in some way the satisfaction of an appetite that could have been spiritual, I would even say one that was meant to be spiritual. The cult of celebrities is thus a cult in something more than a metaphorical sense; it is a displaced cult of what is regarded as the good, the beautiful and the true, through a series of misappropriations and misconceptions more or less willingly entertained. If what I say were not the case, then it would be hard to explain pop idols, *Hello* magazine, fanzines, the semi-religious conservation of the memory of Elvis, who no longer needs a last name, or of Princess Diana, especially after her death. One could in fact learn much from the comparison of Diana and Mother Teresa, who died at the same time, and the way that their deaths were received and their memory preserved. Nearly everything that has been said about Mother Teresa has recognised that she lived and died for her faith and for her love of Jesus Christ, that this was the explanation for her life of self-sacrifice and why she is able to offer a model for others. In the case of Diana, however, nearly everything that has been said by her adulators has been about her personality, her emotions, her adventures, her sufferings. This minute examination of Diana goes nowhere; it is utterly pointless, other than its being able to satisfy a sentimental and insatiable public appetite.

How then does one judge this phenomenon of the cult of *celebs*? Is it just a harmless pastime for the bored? Some might think that it is as valid a way of entertaining one's imagination as a religious meditation. Or they might consider it a deformation of the spiritual instinct. Not only am I convinced that it is largely the latter, but it also seems evident that such preoccupations or obsessions are harmful to our spiritual natures. They take up too much space in people's minds; they lull the imagination so that it does not seek substance with more fruitfulness; they engage perverse curiosity and vicarious strivings that are corrupting, and they breed indifference to any transcendent reality by squeezing it out of consciousness. Perhaps no one thinks that celebs are gods, but they could be described as false gods.

Youth culture – Sociological studies of youth have made us aware of the distinctiveness of the youth culture of our time, globalised through the effects of mass media and advertising, and separated from the mainstream of society. It is the media that carries images and information about its icons, and reflects and mediates the culture to its members. Indeed it frequently exists as a virtual culture, one that comes into existence through the media or at events, such as raves, matches or gigs, and exists much of the rest of the time in people's imaginations and fantasies.[3] A whole culture of the young has become massively visible, through the influences of fashion, music, and changing patterns of values and behaviour. If the young are seduced by the accoutrements of fashion, by living with a certain lifestyle, using alcohol and drugs freely, disregarding values that might be seen as traditional, relating to family, sexual behaviour, denying respect to other people's beliefs, rights, property, and so forth, as current social surveys suggest, then they have lost their roots and become vulnerable to sudden shifts in ideas that are aimed at further subordination of the young to particular market or political interests or the blandishments of false religions and sects which promise new freedoms and special knowledge.

There is an agenda of refusal by a significant proportion of the young to accept the status quo, the belief systems of a previous age that are being offered to them by a diminishing proportion of an older generation. There is little interest in the old rituals of social life, or in the discoveries and choices made by a previous generation. There is widespread stereotyping of parents as repressive, of public institutions as brainwashing, and of jobs as exploitative. The rites of passage to adulthood are thus ignored or rejected. These perceptions in fact handicap youth. But they handicap society too, and they leave the Church seen as wrong, passé, and irreconcilable with the interests or preferences of youth. In many ways the individual young person is left without a homeland, without a place to belong, except as the participant in an ephemeral event, fashion or group relationship. Music, sex, drink, drugs, clothes, football events, celebs, these are the phenomena that define the passing world, and incite the young to belong. As Scruton puts it, youth becomes a goal in itself, a purpose, not a transition to adulthood.

It is important, however, not to make too one-sided a judgement. If we take the case of the young, it certainly cannot be maintained that most of them do not have positive values. The values of group loyalty, friendship, fairness, sympathy for the underdog, generosity to those in need, not to mention enjoyment of life, of beauty, and of personal achievements, are probably as strong among the young as they have ever been. On the other hand, attitudes of suspicion of authority, distrust of officialdom, refusal of constraints upon personal freedom, and scepticism about traditional guardians of standards of behaviour and morality, such as teachers, the police or the churches, have all probably become stronger than ever before amongst the young. One of the effects of the formation of a youth culture on youth itself is to create a gulf separating the young from other generations, so that they lack models, leaders and sources of values outside their own social groups. This may be construed as freedom from traditional controls, from parental authority, and from any accountability to others, but it also leads to a condition of being culturally adrift, with a short time perspective, and intense and often narcissistic self-preoccupation. The values and attitudes that go along with such perspectives can vary from alienation, rebellion or revolutionary thinking on the one hand, to hyper-individualism, fear of involvement, and self-destructive or despairing loss of meaning on the other.[4]

Scruton notes that youth culture is acknowledged by nearly all as the culture to be fostered.[5] His work is valuable because he is not looking at youth for their own sake but in order to understand how the culture of youth modifies the whole cultural scene, as when everyone begins to seek to ape youth. People of an age which might be thought to have left youth behind want to continue to be associated with the youth culture in fashion and lifestyle and in avoiding accepting the responsibilities of an adult generation for reproduction and the upbringing of the next generation. Even for senior politicians, churchmen, and intellectuals, let alone ageing pop-stars, youth is the new elite. The difference is that youth is not an achievement but a state, a being locked into the present, like Princess Diana. What is happening is that a whole society is seeking to rejuvenate itself. This is a metaphysical process or, in psychological terms, a kind of existential concern about the way reality is seen to be and the goals to which people aspire.

The spiritual search - The genuine spiritual seeker is someone who is looking for the ultimate, in truth, meaning, beauty, and in what feels good. We talk about the feel-good factor with a different sense of the word good, but perhaps this is part of the displacement. A shaky sense of the good, the beautiful and the true could perhaps lead someone to a false conclusion, the selection of a way of life that is not spiritual in itself, but which has emerged from a mistaken search, a frustrated desire, that had something of the absolute in it. What are some of the attributes of this alternative search? It is risk-taking, desperate, total, persistent, sacrificial, testing, probing, and longing for the satisfaction of a completely meaningful response. Maybe it is not so far from the genuinely spiritual; it has many of the same attributes, but it gets lost in its trajectory, ending up immersed in self rather than in communion with the Other.

At an abstract level this seems plausible enough, but what about where it is the case of the young person perpetually drug-taking or bingeing, deliberately seeking a nirvana of drunkenness, unable to see the loss of dignity, the danger to health, the self-absorption, the dead-end character of the experience of sex, drugs, alcohol or self-indulgent hedonism? Compare this with the monk in contemplative prayer, the spiritual trance, the peace of heart and mind, the absorption into God, the personal conviction and commitment, the certainty of finding something that will never disappoint in all eternity. There is something of a parallel in the two uncompromising dispositions, but they will not be able to understand one another, because each will think they have made the only possible choice, because neither could make the choice that the other has made. Who is right? Or who can decide who is right? It is a matter of belief. How can one be changed into the other? Only by changing the inherent belief in the type of abandonment of self that can take one furthest. Each can try to convince the other, and in a relativist perspective either can succeed. But in a realist perspective it is a question of how a person who is destroying him or herself can be brought to perceive that there is an alternative, because there is a truth. Occasionally, though, there is a break through, and a dazed seeker emerges into a truly illuminated state, often with an absorbing story to tell. [6]

One mysterious feature of the culture of youth today is the fact that some young people are fascinated by New Age and oriental spirituality, while totally rejecting what they see as traditional Christianity, while others seem equally inclined to be totally sceptical, materialistic, and indifferent to the spiritual. Why should these two alternatives coexist? We will return to the spiritual option later, but can observe here that the materialistic and hedonistic tendencies to be observed among the young are not simply the product of their own thinking. Huge commercial interests are involved in marketing consumer goods to the young, and deliberate efforts are made to persuade them to adopt the appropriate possessions for a lifestyle built on certain prevailing but extremely transient values, such as staying ahead, being cool, proving one's elders wrong, doing one's own thing and finding one's own way. Whole industries strive to change the behaviour of young people and to condition them to conformity. Oppositional forces are arrayed against families, schools and churches to win the minds and hearts of the young. Not to recognise this is to take an extremely implausible view of young people as self-determining; it is indeed to espouse the naively over-confident view they so often take of themselves, until the moment comes when they they have sadly to acknowledge: 'I just can't stop myself'. [7]

NOTES

[1] Nichols, p.16

[2] cf. in the works of the biologist Richard Dawkins, such as *The Selfish Gene*. Oxford: OU Press, 1989: and *The God Delusion*. London: Bantam, 2006.

[3] note Scruton, op.cit., Chapter 9: 'Yoofanasia'

[4] cf. Nick Pollard, *Why do they do that? Understanding Teenagers*. Oxford: Lion Publishing, 1998

[5] Scruton, p. 100.

[6] cf. John Pridmore with Greg Watts, *From Gangland to the Promised Land*. Stoke on Trent: Alive Publishing, 2004.

[7] Pollard, op. cit., p.112.

CHAPTER FIVE

Exposing Moral Relativism

GOSPEL TRUTH IS now accepted by only a minority, perhaps a small minority, of humanity. Human society is afflicted by the results of its rebellion against God, some of the spiritual fruits of which are unbelief, conflict and death. The rejection of the Gospel cannot be definitive, since it is the basic truth about humanity and its destiny. Human history is a struggle between light and darkness, and it is somehow ironical that what was called the Enlightenment has been the cause of such darkness. Scruton aptly summarises this process. First, reason made a claim over and above faith, and virtue was asserted independently of the ultimate source of good. Then the arts and literature became the chosen means to provide the secular sanctity that is civilisation. In time, the power of reason and civilisation was challenged as bourgeois by the postmodernists, who are able to pursue relativism to its ultimate, where there is no longer any meaning other than the 'No meaning' they assert. Continuing the process of upending the traditions that had come from belief in God, and especially from Christianity, the structures of society are rejected, especially structures of power, but also constraining influences on pleasure-seeking. Sexual freedom is proclaimed, marriage is undermined, and morality is relativised. This allows youth to claim authority, the future to be rejected as much as the past, children as much as parents, and nihilism takes over through incessant self-reference and idolatry of the symbols that legitimise or express the rights of self, and yet there develop a willingness to self-destruct through addictions, a refusal to earn a place in adult society, mantras of forgetfulness in music, dance and humour, and in the end the terrible meaninglessness of suicide pacts. As Scruton says, when the power that is asserted is based upon the evacuation of shared meaning it is 'the world of the Devil'.[1] St Paul, revolted by the evidence of the idolatry of the Athenians, identifies the errors of pagan religion.

Step two
Exposing the moral relativism that obscures Christian truth

If Christians are to find seeds of the Gospel in secular cultures they have to be deliberate in their observation, approach and criticisms, and yet clearly confront differences in beliefs and values. However, no effective discussion can occur without a language or approach that is sensitive enough to accommodate both the spiritual and the secular, for example, to speak of and explain Scripture or to reveal Jesus unstereotypically and imaginatively in a world that takes a postmodern worldview for granted. Secular worldviews cannot simply be rejected out of hand. The Christian is obliged by his own faith to approach those of other beliefs with the respect due to sincere persons, but then go on to offer correction and appropriate reasoning to counter negative views of faith and of religious understandings of the world. A meeting place, sometimes called by Pope John Paul a modern Areopagus, is needed for believers and unbelievers, and modes of engagement to guide their interactions, so that the conflictual does not dominate, or turn the discussion into active cultural warfare. From this process, either through the transformation of cultures from within or through reconciliation between faith and culture, a more global and humanistic approach to values and meanings can be fostered, and a hearing gained for the gospel message.

The culture of death and the civilisation of love

Some of the most important values in human life relate to how we live with each other, and how we relate both socially and sexually. Involved in this is our sense of our own identity, our model of humanity, our view of the main purposes of human life, and the value we attach to the human being. Following from this is our understanding of the meaning and purpose of sexual relations, and our responsibility for each other in all social relations including sexual, as well as the higher values of sacrifice, self-donation and fidelity to the religious creed that ascribes value to the other as made in the image of God. Other relationships are derived from this model, because we understand humanity as in effect one family, under the fatherhood of God, with all people brothers and sisters of each other. The Christian injunction to love our neighbour is simply the practical implication of this belief and its natural expression in relationship.

Flowing from this basic principle of love and respect for each human being, and for life itself as the gift of the Creator, are many implications that affect how we see and behave towards one other. Thus, since in the Catholic understanding the human person begins life at conception, it is clear that the Church must completely reject induced abortion of all kinds. However, the same principle binds the Christian conscience in all use of sexuality, since it is from the intentions with which we use our sexuality that life-giving consequences flow. To use sexuality but to block its consequences is to fail in this respect, and to fail in a grave matter.

To speak of human rights without acknowledging the rights of the unborn is a logical failure, an injustice, and a moral failing, and yet this is the position of what is probably a substantial majority of people in contemporary society, certainly in the West, and even many who as cafeteria Catholics pick out only those precepts that they are prepared to observe. If contemporary culture has taken a morally flawed course in such a major respect, it is hardly surprising that all kinds of moral consequences have ensued to create a secular materialistic ethic that can no longer be reconciled with Christian faith. Short of conversion, the secular materialist has excluded him- or herself from a holistic ethic of human relationships, and it is from this flawed first step that many moral evils of our time, such as pornography, promiscuity, injustice, oppression, and war, inevitably follow.

Chastity, a notion that has been little more than a joke in the recent past, is now taken much more seriously in the United States and in some African countries scourged by Aids. Notable converts from the abortion industry and its advocacy have shocked those who assumed that only their view could prevail. And resistance to viewing homosexual partnerships as an acceptable alternative to heterosexual marriage remains strong. This has appeared both symbolically in the American Episcopalian Church and in the Catholic Church, with awareness of its potential consequences for the priesthood, and more broadly in the opposition from African and Muslim societies that have no place for homosexual activity.

Briefly characterised, these are conflicts between those who see human life materialistically, something that can be controlled and managed like any other natural resource, and those who see human life as a special creation of God in his own image, and thus of infinite value, and worthy of the respect due to its Creator. One approach leads to biological experimentation, contraception, abortion and euthanasia, while the other leads to the cherishing of human life from conception to natural death, the acceptance of new life as a gift from God, and a favouring of policies that lead to sharing as widely as possible the blessings of a civilisation of love, including economic, social, political, medical, and especially spiritual, benefits.

In his writings Pope John Paul spoke frequently of a culture of death which has come to characterise those secular societies of the modern era that have accepted abortion, euthanasia, in vitro fertilisation, embryo experimentation and eugenics.[2] All this is justified by appeal to benefits that such measures bring: reducing excess population, protecting women from the stress of too many children, giving people freedom, accepting people's desire to end their lives painlessly and with dignity when their medical condition becomes severe or when they become mentally incapacitated, or finding new ways to heal degenerative diseases by supplying cells that can grow into what the body needs to have restored. What is not accepted is that the cost of all these procedures is the deaths of human beings, and this is why such a self-righteous culture is none the less one of death.

A culture of life or, as the Pope expressed it, a civilisation of love, is in radical contrast. It involves recognition of the right to life, the dignity of every human being from natural conception to the grave, and thus respect for the embryo, the unborn baby, the handicapped child, the dying, and underlying all of this a fundamental attitude of reverence for the Creator and an unwillingness to usurp his role as the arbiter of life. Despite the claims of the advocates of secularism, abortion, euthanasia and the like to be emancipators, there is incomparably more freedom in the Christian vision of the human person made in God's image and destined, according to Scripture, Church teaching and the faith of the believer, to live with God in the fullest expression of his capacities for understanding, enjoyment and love. Pope Benedict XVI, in a book published only days before his election, entitled *Values in a Time of Upheaval*, drew attention to what he said was the need of the West, and especially of Europe, to seek its own soul very consciously. He identified three aspects of this search: human dignity and human rights that have to be given absolute value which precedes any legislative action by the State, acknowledgement of marriage and the family, and, reverence for God. Human dignity is particularly respected in the Christian understanding of marriage and the family and is never in conflict with reverence for the divine.[3]

The cultures of life and death stand opposed to one another in contemporary society. They are irreconcilable, and in the end one must submit to the other. As things stand, the pressure is upon the defenders of life and love to give way, under the force of law and the strength of official opinion expressed through ethical committees in the health services and the like. Yet it is not certain that these views will prevail. The tide of opinion may be turning against abortion and sexual promiscuity just when legal systems are being reorganised to facilitate both, for example by extending the conditions under which abortions can be performed and permitting the distribution of the morning-after pill to young people without the knowledge of their parents.

It could be said that there is a vast movement whose logic is self-destruction, through the chain of developments that undermine life, set reproduction on one side, and separate sexual activity from procreation. In vitro fertilisation cannot rival natural methods of procreation. It is notoriously inefficient, and it is death-dealing much more than it is life-giving because it has led to the destruction of so many embryos. In so many ways, by an evil concentration of apparently different causes, it is the human race that is being destroyed. Birth rates have fallen far below the levels required to sustain current population levels in large numbers of countries. The likely long-term implications of this are hardly being thought about: their consequences for the elderly in the future, the mass migrations that must follow, the mental illness and depression that will afflict those who do not fulfil their biological (and biblical) calling to increase and multiply, and the falling levels of economic growth due to the dwindling of the labour force. In those countries which have allowed selective abortion on grounds of sex, or even the abandoning of unwanted female infants, the consequences in the long term include large excesses of males, aggressive competition for females, sexual assaults on women and children, diseases, militarism, and other social, economic and political instabilities.

Basic human rights are advocated by all enlightened people, but do we see all the implications? The most fundamental human right in all logic is the right to life, and the next most important is the right to one's own beliefs insofar as they do not adversely infringe on other people. This is the argument for life, but it is also the argument against the pro-choice position. It depends upon seeing the unborn as a human being, and beyond that a human person, though no one can in fact convincingly separate these two, as the empty justifications of partial-birth abortion demonstrate. The right of the unborn to life and the denial of a mother's right to choose the death of the child in her womb are two sides of the same coin. The influence of the pro-choice position is largely due to the powerful advocacy of well-educated and articulate people, especially women, while the unborn have only the Catholic Church to speak for them. I say 'only' the Catholic Church, not because the Church is small in numbers or influence, but because it can be made to look as if its position is dictated by the clergy rather than a directly interested party, as with pro-choice women. But this is a misconception. It is becoming increasingly clear that for ordinary Catholics this is a deciding issue: it is self-evident that it is implausible to claim Catholic faith and pro-choice convictions simultaneously, as the conflicts in the US over pro-choice political candidates receiving communion in Catholic churches have shown.

Faith and science – Contemporary society much more easily accepts the truth claims of science than those of religion. Science can, and frequently does, accuse faith of having no empirical basis for its postulates, but it is no less true that faith can question where science is going if it is simply a self-generating process. Why are doing, making and understanding good in themselves, especially if experience shows that understanding is often not cumulative because it follows so many cul-de-sacs and byways, and in any case it produces nothing that can be called wisdom by which we can evaluate what we are doing, or what we should do? Many perceive science as a loose cannon. It dehumanises as much as it humanises. It destroys life as much or more than it saves life through wars, eugenics, abortion, and the irreversible destruction of the living environment. The common reproach to science is: just because something can be done it doesn't mean it should be done.

Reason tells us that science proves nothing, it only disproves, leaving various degrees of probability behind for its theories. We know nothing as a scientific absolute; we only suppose or assert probabilities. Or, to take the argument a little further, if I am not a specialist of the particular subject matter, science actually teaches me nothing directly, and what I might claim it teaches me is only what accredited scientists tell me it teaches, or only what scientists can convince each other that it teaches. Science is merely an invented system of ideas, kept in being by an ongoing process of enquiry which quickly collapses if the enquiry stops, because its propositions atrophy and fail to take account of new conditions and data. In his work on *The Structure of Scientific Revolutions*, Kuhn describes how it has continually happened in the history of scientific thought that a major theoretical discovery has invalidated much that was previously taken for granted.[4] Science then has to begin afresh with a new paradigm or organising framework of ideas. In sum, scientific theory works in terms of approximating to the truth; it cannot tell us the truth.

In science, therefore, and even in religion tarred by the scientific brush, it has become increasingly unfashionable to assert anything called truth. The preference is for opening up new questions and developing fresh methods of enquiry. There is little publicly acknowledged hope of reaching answers. In fact, scientists are worse off than religious believers because they accept that their findings are dependent upon their methods of enquiry whereas traditional religious believers trust that there is a truth, even if it is not fully accessible. The initiative lies with the hidden God who may or may not decide to reveal the truth. A religious person who does not believe this is a fraud. Such a person is a scientist in disguise.

Political correctness – Another conventional source of truth in contemporary society, at least in terms of how easily it gains authority, is political correctness. Recently I heard an American feminist speak disparagingly of political correctness. She implied that it was a term used by unthinking people to dismiss views that they were not willing to do the hard work of understanding, and presumably accepting. She was convinced that her view should prevail. Perhaps this is the essence of it, the stance of certain people, usually secularist in mentality, whose opinions have become the dogmas of secular society. I think of radical feminists, extremist political groups, as well as opinion-leaders and senior media people, high status academics, some clerics and inclusive language enthusiasts, members of certain pressure groups, and ideologues of many hues. This kind of blind reasoning is very prevalent, especially on gender issues, but also in matters touching faith. It becomes PC not so much to espouse atheism as to disparage the tenets of faith, to mock its simplicity, its unquestioningness, and above all its morality. Another of the characteristic dogmas is 'freedom', taken as meaning the refusal of any system of rules or absolute values, particularly in the sexual area. This is nothing other than a secular fundamentalism.

The paradoxical situation arises that the denizens of political correctness see themselves as defenders of justice, rights, liberty and rationality, when they are in practice intolerant to the point of being totalitarian, as Pope John Paul pointed out in his encyclical letter *Veritatis Splendor*. Certain things cannot be said, must not be said, and extreme forms of control, to the point of sacking journalists who are not biddable, or editing their stories, and neglecting to report news that does not fit their political prescriptions, are unscrupulously and flagrantly practised, since those who control the media do not have to report on their own injustices and failings in integrity.[5] Political correctness breeds fear and conformism, and thus leads directly to injustice and oppression. This line of reasoning is characteristic also of Pope Benedict XVI, who in his last homily before his election to the papacy said:

> *Having a clear faith, according to the Creed of the Church, is often labelled as fundamentalism. While relativism, in other words allowing oneself to be 'tossed to and fro with every wind of doctrine', appears as the only attitude appropriate to modern times, a dictatorship of relativism is being formed, one that recognises nothing as definitive and that has as its measure only the self and its desires.* [6]

In a similar manner, radical as opposed to soundly Christian feminists, whether or not they claim to be Catholics, are those whose monocular vision allows them to raise their self-interest to the level of an ideology, an intellectual construction that is actually harmful to women socially, biologically and spiritually.[7] The inadequacy of the approach appears not in its basic principles but in its extremes, as for example in the matter of inclusive language, where political correctness leads to contortions of syntax and ludicrous assumptions, even though the basic principle of ensuring that women are given equal respect is valid. While some element of truth subsists in their ideology of victimhood as the result of genuine personal hurt suffered, and also the hope of remedy that has been awakened, there is little left of Christian faith in the redemption promised by Jesus. Socially, their despising of men (even proposing gendercide!) and of families has seriously negative consequences for social stability and child-rearing. It becomes impossible to speak of such a thing as a feminine quality, and therefore gentleness, tender love, maternal care, patience, nurturing and so many other essential human qualities, common of course to both sexes while traditionally much more common to women, come not only to be treated as insignificant, but to be despised. Biologically, such feminists harm the race by separating sexuality from child-bearing and espousing pro-choice stances, and spiritually, they lose the Christocentric vision of Christianity, offer a derogatory understanding of the Virgin Mary, and assume the rebellious attitudes characteristic of spiritual warfare.

While this may extend the normal range of the term 'political correctness', what I am looking for is what characterises the phenomenon in its advocates. It seems to me that one finds arrogance, intellectualism, obsession with winning an argument, blinkeredness, and often a personal sense of slight or injustice. The issues they focus on, such as inequality, discrimination, and human rights, are not necessarily bad causes, but their tunnel vision impels them to make their perspective the only one seen as worthy of intelligent people. Thus, all inequalities and often even distinctions between men and women, real or imaginary, have to be rooted out, whatever their history, and whatever contrary views are to be found. A thought-police mentality governs their censorship of words, pronouns, expressions, idioms, and behaviours that might be interpreted as accepting anything other than their, often arbitrary, view. Like relativists and postmodernists who posit notions that are incompatible with their own baseless vision of reality, political correctness advocates are building their houses on sand. One is left with the sense that their conviction is all the more strongly urged because of the lack of any firm foundation they can claim for it. Indeed, in his assessment of contemporary values, Pope Benedict has suggested that there is a form of pathological self-hatred to be found in the West. The rationalists' commitment to freedom of thought does not extend to the freedom to cherish its own Christian historical roots. Here is where one of the ideas that have been most intriguingly associated with the beginning of Pope Benedict's pontificate is advanced:

> '*Believing Christians should conceive of themselves as a creative minority. They should also contribute so that Europe can once again benefit from the best of its inheritance and the whole of mankind will thus be served.*[8]

Post modernism and false prophets

Postmodernism is the ideology that reconciles all things by welcoming every style of thought and every value that has adherents, but obscures its own nihilistic agenda. It is simply a theory within the humanities, but one that affects theology and indeed spirituality and faith itself. One can conceptualise its development in sociological terms. It is a typical academic rebellion against the status quo, in that it attempts to undermine the prevalent rationalism or modernism.[9] It does this by seeking to redefine the concepts and tools of enquiry in the humanities. This methodological innovation is a tactic, but is claimed to be a theory, the theory that all truth is relative, that only the meaning being exchanged at the present moment is valid, though of course it then becomes invalid with the passage of time, or when viewed by other actors who are not involved in the specific conversation or enquiry.

It cannot be denied that many of these same processes have affected the Church, so that theology and spirituality have themselves been challenged, and their advocates have sometimes lost their footing to subjectivity, experiential approaches and fashionable ideologies. This sociological context of ecclesial change has been described very effectively by Flanagan, especially as it affects liturgy and theological studies, but the implications go much further. Career-mindedness among theologians puts theology on the same footing as any other discipline, and thus the doctrinal and moral character of their work is compromised. Radical relativism, as Flanagan points out, becomes a tool in the hands of those academics who are best able to articulate the theory. This does not mean the best articulation from the rational point of view, as Scruton demonstrates through his critique of texts from postmodern authors. Instead what emerges is an almost military campaign of deconstruction, one could say iconoclasm, as every contrary viewpoint is undermined, and a new orthodoxy is established. The sequence is one of power-seeking, and the powerful are those who are able to impose their line of thought, the line of thought that says that there is no valid thought outside of the expression of it at a particular point in time or space. Or, according to Jacques Derrida's famous dictum: 'There is no meaning outside of the text.'

Postmodernism, once entertained, becomes a kind of virus that destroys discourse, and one that especially infects all traditional thinking and values, all orthodoxies, faiths and absolutes. Some have sought to live with this, finding a new freedom in exploration, but necessarily in a seeking without finding. We need to question those artists and writers who seem to have lost a sense of seeking anything they actually expect can be found. Have they reached the point where there is no point to their activities other than to enhance their own status, name or reputation? What is even more important for us to note is the sociological revelation that relativism is a strategy that is self-destructive, since its truth must also by its own theory be relative. The same restrictions do not bind realist perspectives, since they contain within themselves the proviso that they must bend to new evidence which it is posited will take the enquiry closer to the truth, or nearer to finding out about ways of approaching the truth that always subsists independently of the stance of the enquirer. Sociology is needed in intellectual history if we are not to be incapacitated in such a way as to fail to recognise what we are doing when we marginalise the supernatural, dismiss the objective, overemphasise the contemporary, the actual, the experiential, and neglect the enduring fears and anxieties of 'post-Christian' society.

Once people have lost confidence in rationality, in absolutes, in any universal meaning and purpose, all that is left is each person's garnerings out of experience and conversation. And yet the knowledge that one can change one's mind with changing situations or new elements of experience means that one can have no faith even in one's present knowledge; one can have no conviction and no commitment. This is in fact what many live, except that most have some kind of lingering idea of integrity that keeps them from living the utter logic of their position, which would be to be completely amoral, totally selfish, and fundamentally solipsistic. Or it could be that a sense of pride makes people not want to appear inferior to others in virtue as society defines it at a particular point in time, and perhaps this is what political correctness is: the clutching hold of a semblance of virtue, all the more savagely adhered to precisely because it protects from the ghastly recognition that there is nothing else, no certainty, no basis for any commitment, nothing but make-believe.

There is in effect a tension between two views of reality, and one of them appears to the Christian to be an illusion, a virtual reality that threatens to take over, a psychological trap that encapsulates more or less willing victims like Cipher in the film, *The Matrix*, or a suspension of belief accompanied by an angst of the spirit, as I thought I detected in the exhibition of the work of Chagall I mentioned earlier which seemed so emblematic of the 20th century -- a knowing that the mundane reality being assumed is incomplete because we keep needing to enhance it, vary it, reconfigure it, or imagine it otherwise, while all the time ignoring the piece of the jigsaw puzzle that makes the whole pattern clear. And it is this very culture, with its dominant strains of secularism, individualism, relativism and postmodernism, that the Christian living in fidelity to the Gospel is called to evangelise.

False prophets – The false prophet is not just the familiar prophet of doom, who looks on the worst side of things, or attempts to provoke fear of consequences of a dire kind.[10] What is being referred to here is rather the person who is malevolent, deceptive, consciously seeking to mislead, to seduce, to lead into error and sin, or the immoral fashions, trends and doctrines that seduce. After all, often when we follow someone it is because of their ideas, not simply their charm. And what is false about false prophets may be their inherent treachery, deceit, evil intentions, and so forth, but it can equally be their teachings, their ideas, their priorities, their deceitful visions, or the panoply of pseudo-religion that they have used to ensnare others.

The phrase is used in Matthew, Chapter 7, to mean false teachers of religion, but it can be used to mean any teacher about life, values, or crucial issues who is ultimately opposed to the interests of the people he addresses, such as cult leaders, gurus of the music and drug scene, and media personalities who argue for alternative marriages, abortion and other such self-destructive causes. In his work, *Architects of the Culture of Death*,[11] Donald de Marco explores the harmful traditions of thought which have been developed by philosophers, psychiatrists, sexologists, radical political thinkers and others who have often been extremely damaged and unhappy people themselves, but who have managed to find an echo in people's needs and desires, though in fact they undermine them by putting them on a road to nowhere, or even to damnation. This is the broad road, usually not demanding, fitting in with people's weaknesses, but also sometimes subjecting them to psychological slavery so that a lot can be demanded of them in discipline, obedience and work, as is the case, for example, of Jehovah's Witnesses.

False prophets, then, are those who seek to build kingdoms that are not of the Lord. It is the opposite motivation to that of the one who announces the good news of salvation. Where God makes a promise according to his covenant, the false prophet seeks to convince that there is another reward or way that corresponds more closely to a person's hopes or interests. They deny the truth of Christ or deliberately work against God. This is not to say that they always understand fully what they are doing. Who knows if Mohammed intended to destroy Christianity? It does not alter the fact that for Christians he is a false prophet. It is no doubt true, however, that the worst false prophets have been those who are perfectly aware of what they are doing, those who use every stratagem to deceive, to mislead, to corrupt, to kidnap psychologically, to reduce resistance, to arouse hostility to the faith. False prophets are not necessarily seeking to be religious leaders, of course. They may intend simply to inflate their own importance by taking over power and authority in society through the influence of their message, even the message of pleasure, nirvana or materialism. Timothy Leary, the American drug-addicted guru of the 1960s was of this kind. He sought to lead people to imitate him, and for a while he had a cult following, but there was nothing to it but indulgence in a drug-induced lifestyle of self-absorption and irresponsibility.

The false prophet can however be very skilful in his approach, just as the message he preaches can be powerful in its influence and its capability for deception and seduction. Not only do we need to be aware of such corruptive influences but we may need to see how they operate, since it is obvious that many such prophets have effectively seduced large numbers of young people in contemporary society, and have led them to a position where they often seem inaccessible to Christian influence. What is happening to such people? They are evidently finding something that appears at the time to be meaningful to them, whether it is pleasure, a social philosophy, a way of relating and living, a conviction that they possess some truth that others have not been able to understand, or a confidence that they no longer need to look to conventional faiths or social doctrines since these have been superseded.

TPAC pulls no punches in speaking of how contemporary society is aggressively combatting the faith:

*An anthropocentric pragmatic atheism, blatant religious
indifference, all-embracing hedonistic materialism are
marginalising the faith, making it appear evanescent,
lacking in cultural substance and relevance.* (TPAC, 7)

An example of such secularism is shown in a Times
interview with Jonathan Miller arrogantly and simplistically
asserting his atheism. He is said by the interviewer to be
'disinventing' God. What he is doing is the opposite of the
evangelising of culture; he wants to do away with the
supernatural vision of life, to institute an atheisation of
culture. Such commentators freely use the term
fundamentalist in their attacks, but it appears that anyone
asserting any truth is a fundamentalist.[12] This tendency, often
encountered amongst atheists and members of such bodies as
the National Secular society, brooks no denial. It is what
communist regimes sought by criminalising religion through
repressive laws throughout the USSR and other societies.
This is the exact opposite of what Christians are called to do,
by disinventing the secularist, atheistic solutions to the
problem of life's meaning and purpose.

There may none the less be common ground between
believers and unbelievers, once we actually sort out what
they believe and disbelieve. Atheism is not itself a faith, but
a belief. It is a good idea to question an unbeliever closely as
to what he thinks Christians believe. Where there may be

more difficulty is in moving from the notion that we should be willing to empathise with atheists, when on examination we find it appropriate, to the inclusion of atheism in school curricula, which has recently been urged in England. To enforce something like this is to give official backing to relativism, if not atheism itself, and to make it very difficult for any social group or faith community to sustain its traditions against universal scepticism. Individual viewpoints cannot have the same rights as an established body of thinking and believing, something sanctioned by society over a period of time, or we are entering into a severely relativistic state where nothing has precedence over anything else: no ideas, no values, no customs or traditions. Furthermore, children, much more than adults, need time to absorb what they are learning, because they have much slenderer foundations. To pour down their throats every kind of belief and disbelief is to ensure that they retain little and believe nothing. This is why it is a better idea to allow them to follow family traditions, given of course that they are not traditions that society needs to be protected from, and then to offer gradual opportunities for a broadening of their learning and a challenge to their ideas that are appropriate to both their age and intelligence.

All that has been referred to as 'false prophets' requires spiritual discernment. In such areas as secular materialistic creeds, neo-paganism or New Age beliefs, postmodern theology building from New Age, ethical relativism, dissent and activism, as well as the occult, eugenics, ecologism, animal rights and green issues, discernment should emphasise both positives and negatives, but collectively would occasion a spiritual wake-up call. It would be difficult to address these points without offending political correctness, but it is very important that this is done, because contemporary culture turns spiritual reality on its head by discussing moral and religious options as if ultimately they can be introduced to suit people's passing interests and convenience.

Bias in the media – It appears indisputable that, by certain strong tendencies to a monopoly of information, championing of secular values, scepticism regarding the truth, and antagonism for Christian faith, the media frequently act to undermine religious belief. The main value espoused is freedom, but this is corrupted, since everybody has 'rights' but there is no 'right'. This is illustrated by the prevalence in the media of moral relativism, pornography, consumerism, erotic advertising and fashions, hedonism as a model of lifestyle, dealing with the stereotypes of machismo and feminine beauty, fascination with the occult and New Age, exaggerated attention to social crises and dysfunctions, a pessimistic outlook on life, continual images of sex and violence, the persistent attitudes of satire, spiritual rebellion and secularist thinking.

When the intention to broadcast *Jerry Springer, the Opera*

was announced in Britain in late 2004, there was a strong reaction, particularly from Christians. While the BBC claimed that the work was cutting-edge musical drama, and that it would be wrong to allow bigoted views to prevent its being seen by discerning viewers, religious and other groups protested that its obscene language and its blasphemy directed at Christ and his mother made it intolerable. There was no dialogue, just anger and bland non-response. It was unconvincing for the BBC to deny anti-Christian prejudice in the production, but the weakness of Christians showed in their failure to achieve its cancellation. In his 2005 document, *The Rapid Development*, the Pope urged Catholics to take up this struggle, by emphasising the moral responsibilities of the media; they are not free to make light of truth and justice:

> *An authentically ethical approach to using the powerful*
> *communication media must be situated within the context*
> *of a mature exercise of freedom and responsibility,*
> *founded upon the supreme criteria of truth and justice.*
> (RD, 3)

The idea that through the modern media we now belong to a global village is an illusory metaphor. It is not a true village but a virtual reality. Though it does have immediate communication links reaching nearly everyone, many of these links are essentially one-way. While potentially every agenda has access to the media, there is obvious bias in programme content according to the decisions made by media owners and producers. While thinking we have global communication, we risk being at the mercy of commercial, political and even cultural interests. The classic image of the media consumer is the faceless member of the public, the passive 'couch potato' who ends his day half-asleep in front of the small screen, absorbing media contents gullibly and uncritically. We do not have a global village in the sense of a community where people know each other, and can relate face to face and evaluate intuitively what they are encountering. It is even dangerous to think like this, because then one will not realise what is really going on, that is, how one is being caught up in a tide, influenced for the worse, like the people who become addicted to television so that it blanks out flesh and blood relationships, or, worse still, creates electronically based obsessions with sex, pornography and other evils. The purification of culture is a task facing Christians that appears publicly when, for example, an art exhibition includes blasphemous or degrading material that makes no worthy contribution to art or culture. The criteria that Christianity brings to bear can be helpful, since society's criteria are so feeble and confused.

There is a literature on bias in the media, but it is not extensive because media professionals protect themselves from such allegations. Yet in the recent past, with the Hutton enquiry in England and the accusations brought by the

Catholic Archbishop of Birmingham against the BBC, it is clear that there is no smoke without fire. There is arrogance in the media as well as a self-righteousness that comes from the dominance of politically correct views among the vast majority of its personnel. Being nearly all on the same side they find it hard to consider any alternative. Recent examples in the media include a BBC programme on contraception and the Vatican that sought very hard to make Vatican officials look foolish, US media treatment of the clerical sex abuse scandal and Irish anti-clericalism in the media which have made innocent priests feel like pariahs, the common refusal to use spokespersons for orthodox Christianity, and the arrogant self-righteousness and prejudice identified by Goldberg in the American CBS television network.[13]

There is some evidence in Goldberg's work that media people are in a sociological sense self-reproducing. They recruit each other, and it is hard for non-conformists to their way of thinking to get anywhere in the media professions. The same is most probably true for Britain. So many in the media are the 20- or 30-somethings, unattached or cohabiting, the intelligentsia who are the advocates of a new morality, or an anti-morality in many respects and certainly in the sexual sphere. There is likely enough a strong homosexual tendency in this subculture, to judge by the increasing incidence of gay presence and advocacy in media content, such as the much hyped 'first gay kiss' in *The Archers* or the introduction of a gay *Sex in the City* series. A clue lies in the high level of indignation that TV interviewers often display when questioning those who have 'conservative' views on sexuality and homosexuality.

All of these issues arising in the media that cause so much damage to the image of the Church and handicap the work of proclaiming the faith effectively are matters that need to concern faithful Christians practically. Protests at misinformation, blasphemies, obscenities, bias, and failures to report Church events, such as World Youth Days that involve millions of people, are justly to be mounted. Experiments with events aimed at gaining the interest of non-believers in ethical and religious causes and dialogues, or in joining in with secular humanitarian efforts in development aid work, Amnesty International or peace-making initiatives, are truly part of any Christian apostolate.

False spirituality – There is a distinction to be drawn between a so-called spirituality that is godless, and a spirituality that takes its reality from the life shared by human beings with God. Spirituality in this latter sense implies the divine, and I contest the notion of any other spirituality which is not a psychologism or a merely aesthetic view of reality. Why call something spiritual unless it partakes of godly life, that is, unless it goes beyond the sphere of human control? If we say that there is some pervasive entity called spirit, but which is not God, or which is a non-self-conscious, non-being but none the less exerting power over human beings, I wonder what it could possibly be other than a stunted view of the transcendent God.

Our godless culture wants some halfway house, a god that is not God, so that it can appear to be all-inclusive, so that it can encompass the claims of the religious, but redefine them as self-generated needs and dependencies. This allows humans to assume a full autonomy, to become gods for themselves. They may claim that the power lies in nature, and may seek to reveal this power through experiments and rituals, but such pagan features merely obscure the prideful effort to place the human above any possibility of divine transcendence. Words like spiritual and divine are thus apt to be misused because faith in a divine being is not faith in self, but in the wholly Other, an entity that as Creator has power of initiative, and not a derivative being who would have no reality unless there were a pre-existent human society to generate it. Pagan New Age spirituality is of this latter kind. It apes transcendent spirituality by its apparent high-mindedness, its seeking to go beyond the individual, to find some shared experience or power that then acts back upon the person. But this is an illusion if it is not indeed a hostage to fortune, since the power it invites to display itself could well be real, and autonomous, and destructive of human authenticity and autonomy. Believers in a transcendent God recognise the existence of evil as the corrupted behaviour of those who seek to deny, thwart or evade God. A creed that asserts a god that does not know evil, as is the case of the New Age sense of the divine, is thus corrupted from the start.

There is thus a whole range of false spiritualities, from those that have sought salvation in new religions to a neo-paganism or New Age beliefs. And there is a postmodern theology, building from New Age, ethical relativism, dissent and activism, which has often been granted credibility precisely through the moral failures of the wider Church community in its scandals and abuses of power. Practical examples are too numerous to pursue exhaustively but they occur in cults and sects offering a claimed spiritual power and knowledge in such areas as astrology, the occult, Satanism, individualism and moral relativism, strains of liberation theology infused with Marxist ideology, ecumenism marked by doctrinal compromise, fundamentalist sectarianism, sexual liberationism, humanistic psychology, radical feminism and ecologism.

The Pontifical Council for Culture published a most insightful report in 2003 on New Age beliefs.[14] Drawing attention to the pantheistic character common to many of its expressions, the report is illuminating on the way in which a spirituality derived from Eastern religions is adapted to Western concerns, thus managing to combine a strong individualism based on the 'god within' with a holistic and ecologistic identification with what is seen as universal. The denial of a transcendent God, and of the reality of sin and salvation, produces a gulf between New Age and Christianity. Efforts to heal the break between faith and culture by imagining newly synthesised religious forms or compromise solutions that are seen as more 'relevant', or more comprehensible to modern people, only succeed in widening the gulf. This is because the solutions proposed actually compound the problem, because faith and reason are distinct and yet co-essential.

It is not being denied here that there can be a nobility about the seeking for a divine power that has not yet been found. The PCC document notes 'the often silent cry in people's hearts, which leads them elsewhere if they are not satisifed by the Church'.[15] Many people have come to religious faith through a stage of doubt and pondering and gradual enlightenment. But it is one thing to seek God with an open mind and heart, and another to rule out a priori the existence of an omnipotent Deity through pride or self-interest. Coming to know the transcendent God is coming to accept humility, obedience and a spiritual life which are in the image of God. While the postmodern tendency of New Age is to reject rationality, what is needed rather is the 'healthy partnership between faith and reason'.[16] As the report points out, there are many positive aspirations in New Age, or we could say many seeds of the Gospel that could be brought to new growth by Jesus Christ, 'the bearer of the water of life'.

So far the intent has been to indicate, often in stark terms, the expanse of the gap that separates much of contemporary culture from Christian faith. This has not been done in a negative spirit or with an intent to demonise, but it has been important to expose the full extent of the loss of faith that has occurred if we are to find the reasons, the will and the inspiration to energise the contrary movement that is the evangelising of secular culture.

NOTES

[1]Scruton, p. 128.

[2]The main source is the Encyclical, John Paul II, *Evangelium Vitae*.

[3]Benedict XVI, *Values in a Time of Upheaval*. San Francisco, Ignatius Press, 2006

[4]Thomas Kuhn, *The Structure of Scientific Revolutions*. Chicago: U. of Chicago Press, 1970.

[5]Bernard Goldberg, *Bias: a CBS Insider Exposes how the Media distort the News*. New York: Harper/Collins, 2003.

[6]Benedict XVI, in his Mass before the opening of the consistory

[7]Josephine Robinson, *The Inner Goddess: Feminist Theology in the Light of Catholic Teaching*. Leominster: Gracewing, 1998.

[8]Benedict XVI, *Werte...,op.cit.*

[9]Kieran Flanagan, *The Enchantment of Sociology: a Study of Theology and Culture*. Basingstoke: Macmillan, 1996.

[10]Nichols, *Christendom Awake*, p.23

[11]Donald de Marco and Benjamin Wiker, *Architects of the Culture of Death*. San Francisco: Ignatius Press, 2004.

[12]So-called liberal thinkers betray their own fundamentalism in expressing repressive views concerning religion, for example, an article by the well-known British columnist Will Hutton, 'Heed not the fanatics: only by rebutting fundamentalism in all its forms can we stop ourselves being plunged into a new Dark Age' *The Observer,* April 11, 2004.

[13]Goldberg, op. cit.

[14]Pontifical Council for Culture, *Jesus Christ, the Bearer of the Water of Life*. PCC, 1999.

[15]*Jesus Christ, bearer...*, 1.5

[16]*Jesus Christ, bearer...*, 6

CHAPTER SIX

Witnessing to the Gospel

F, IN THE course of a day, I read an article about fasting in a magazine, see a television programme about raising money for earthquake victims, speak with a neighbour about the responsibility they are carrying in caring for an elderly relative, answer the door to Jehovah Witnesses bravely enduring public contempt, and then during a train journey have an agreeable conversation about experiences of corporate life with a stranger or notice a beautiful country church from the train, can I not then let pass some of the political bickering, the highly publicised extramarital adventures of celebrities, and the aggressive gestures of another motorist as I drive home from the station. Will this average day of quite normal experiences not teach me something about what actually works and what does not work in society? Perhaps I will not have discovered immediately what Pope John Paul called the 'spirituality of communion' (see Chapter 10), but I could be headed in the right direction and therefore be open to God's gift of understanding at the time of his choosing.

For the believer, God is everywhere, but the evangelist does not so much need to prove this as to reveal or express it. This work can be conceived of as existing at different levels. The proclamation of the saving work of Jesus Christ is the most basic and indispensable element. Then follows the unveiling of the beauty, order and elaboration of the natural world by which we find the Creator in the things he has made. A further level is the humanly created world of culture, whose images, words and symbols can reflect the divine, as St Paul strove to persuade the Athenian philosophers.

Step three
bearing witness to the good news of salvation

Believers seek to witness to Jesus as Saviour and to what the Gospel proposes regarding both specific issues and as a coherent message of beliefs and ways of life. They recognise God's self-revelation in creation and they are therefore able to find the transcendent in the everyday. By viewing the world in the perspective of eternity they not only recognise and proclaim the primacy of God's action, but are drawn to use their human gifts of creativity and imagination to discern the good, and to draw others' attention to elements of truth, goodness and beauty embedded in the created world and the life of cultures.

Inspired evangelists, that is those who are truly seeking the face of Christ (NMI, 16-28), will discover seeds of his Gospel through their awareness of both people and cultures and their participation in the dialogue between faith and culture.

Telling the Good News – The gospel model for all evangelising is the work of Jesus in proclaiming a new Covenant, which is his sacrificial self-offering for sin and his opening of the way to eternal life for all humanity. What can we learn from any similarities between that time and now? Jesus came to earth as the longed-for Messiah, the one who would lead Israel to the promised Kingdom. But what Jesus offered was not what the people had come to expect, because they had corrupted their vision of the Messianic Kingdom into something earthbound, nationalistic, and limited by the horizons of human thought and understanding. It had been prophesied, notably by Simeon when he met the Holy Family coming into the temple, that Jesus would be a sign of contradiction. This meant that his life and teachings would confound the world of his time, and this in spite of his fulfilment of the prophecies of Isaiah, his miracles of healing, and his amply demonstrated right to call himself the good shepherd, the light of the world, or indeed the way, the truth and the life. Jesus' difficulty with his public mission, foreshadowed in the themes of his temptation in the desert, was precisely that he was offering the people a new vision of the Kingdom. He sought to show that this was the accomplishment of the divine will, since he had come simply and solely to do the will of the Father. But, despite all his teaching in word and in deed, only a few could understand his efforts to meet people's ignorance, fear and suspicion by witness, imaginative stories, symbolic actions, and faithful love carried to unimagined extremes.

Scripture dramatically portrays the confrontation of the new and old Covenants with the mysterious tableau of the Transfiguration. The great figures of the old Covenant, the culture of the Law personified by the lawgiver, Moses, and the prophet who defeats the false prophets of Baal, Elijah, are seen awaiting illumination, and they speak with the resplendently transfigured Jesus about his forthcoming passion in Jerusalem. The voice of God in the cloud says: 'This is my beloved Son; listen to him'. It can be seen in this event that God the Father speaks and the Holy Spirit shines forth in Jesus, so that the Trinity is present to endorse the person, the preaching, and the coming Eucharistic sacrifice and resurrection of the Saviour. The new Covenant is represented in its entirety as the figures of the old Covenant give testimony to the act by which Jesus is to confirm his Messiahship. And not long afterwards, the institution of the Holy Eucharist inaugurates the new and eternal Covenant by which Jesus will be with his disciples always.

Applied to our time, the new Covenant of the Gospel has to be offered to a people entrapped by the 'old', indeed obsolete, law and the false prophets of materialism, rationalism and relativism. The people of today have chosen to stop their ears to the new message, and to declare the autonomy of their reason over the authority of the lawgiver. They have preferred the immediate gratification of earthly honours over the promise of life after death. So, like the ancient Jews, they anthropomorphise their Messiah into an earthly figure and banish the transcendent God from public life. Many further parallels with contemporary culture can be found in the idolatrous behaviour of the Israelites throughout the Old Testament.

Therefore, just like Jesus, Christians of today, the 'Church of the new Covenant' (AG, 4), have to find ways of offering the good news to people who are listening for a very different message, whether it be about sexual or other freedoms, the right to kill the innocent unborn or the helpless old, or the equality of same-sex relationships with marriage between the two sexes created by God and commissioned by him to increase and multiply. Yet, as in the time when Jesus was on earth, the truth of the Gospel does relate exactly to the prophesied Kingdom. The seeds of the Gospel are there in the existing culture, but overgrown by the mosses and fungi of human desires and errors. The task of the apostle is still to proclaim the truth and, where necessary, to give his life in witness to it.

As both Pope Paul and Pope John Paul have said, the world no longer wants words, it wants the witness of deeds and example (EN, 21; TMA, 37). It is always striking how people, even non-believers, respond to genuinely holy persons, as was exemplified during the life and after the death of Mother Teresa, and even more dramatically when Pope John Paul II died. He was known as a witness to Christ, indeed the preeminent one of his time, through his pilgrimages throughout the world, his care for the sick, the way he bore his own sufferings, his forgiving the assailant who sought to assassinate him, and his constant prayerfulness. The lives of such witnesses speak, just as Jesus' did, but that is not the end of the matter. These great efforts have to be followed up by the proclaiming of Jesus as the way, the truth and the life. The kind of discussion of Christianity that occurs in contemporary media is usually so anodyne that it puts people to sleep more than it wakes them up. Even many Christians would rather speak of ideas, or of Christianity, or of human problems, than acknowledge their commitment to the person of Jesus Christ. But contemporary society needs to be more actively challenged by a full proclamation of the living Christ. It is open to any Christian to be a witness for the Gospel. Indeed, it is demanded of them, whether it is in acknowledging their faith before family members, friends, colleagues or in public forums, or in speaking up for moral causes, in proposing to pray for people's needs, in visiting the sick and imprisoned, or in holding vigils outside abortion clinics. All these are spiritual works of mercy since, by putting God first, they ultimately contribute to people's eternal salvation.

Culture infused with faith

The keys to Christian discernment of truth are love and humility. Christians receive these spiritual gifts through grace and in response to prayer. They then run less danger of being discouraged to the point that they can let go of faith. Such risks are most apt to occur when Christians engage in discussions about making the Church more a part of a rational, democratic society in dealing with such issues as contraception, divorce, abortion, homosexuality, bio-medical experiments, euthanasia, premarital sex or, in contrast, such contested aspects of religious life as rituals, ceremonies, sacrifice, penance and atonement for sin through suffering. The human aspect of the Church is contorted by this effort of adjustment, either fearful of becoming irrelevant and useless, or misled by the spirit of compromise, pride or disobedience. The question then arises as to whether the Church is evangelising the world or the world is evangelising the Church. Conversely, with the acceptance of the Gospel, culture is evangelised and elements of the Gospel find their way into common life, as for example in the introduction into political life in Europe of the concepts of *solidarity* and *subsidiarity* that were first developed in papal documents.

Scientists can, if they so choose, make of their science a window on religious mysteries, as St Paul tells us. They can proclaim God by the wonder and brilliance of their discoveries, the intelligence inhering in the universe, and what Teilhard de Chardin called the 'complexification' of creation that leads it not to entropy but to the omega point of Christ.[1] There are several writers, such as Ian Barbour, Alister McGrath and Keith Ward who are responding to the positivist impulse of such atheistic scientists as Peter Atkins, Peter Singer and Richard Dawkins. In *Rebuilding the Matrix*, Alexander writes of the positive relationships between faith and science. Science has been valuable for humanity, but it cannot be made sense of outside of a 'matrix' of meaning which religious thinking and an understanding of culture can provide.[2] More recently Anthony Ricci has provided a discussion of the relationships of philosophy to science, reclaiming the role of realist philosophy in the tradition of Aristotle and Aquinas as a partner of science, by challenging the tendency to accord science authority on its own terms.[3]

Or, if we think of another key group in society, there are an impressive number of young people who are attracted by positive causes, such as helping the victims of famines, or saving wild animals from extinction or forests from destruction, but this does not give the basis for working out a personal value system, let alone a religious worldview. While it is obvious that not all young people are godless secularists, it cannot be denied that there is widespread ignorance of and indifference to religious belief amongst youth in modern society, and that from a Christian standpoint they suffer overwhelmingly from a lack of spiritual awareness and stimulus. It has been remarkable however how enthusiastically young people have responded to such initiatives as the World Youth Days and to the Alpha Course which is intended as an introduction to the Gospel and the Christian faith. Among the virtues of this innovative programme are that it has sought to express itself in the language of everyday life and has been launched in a youth version that targets the young, gathers them as a select group, and offers them a perspective on faith that appears to be culturally accessible to them, even when they may have had no previous exposure to Christianity. To infuse culture with faith was the mission of the apostles, the work of missionaries throughout the ages, and the responsibility of Christian people today, whether or not they are commissioned to preach the Gospel in a formal sense as clergy, religious or members of apostolic organisations.

A positive response to the media – There can be little doubt that the media offer an immense potential resource to the evangelist. However, it is one thing to know about the media, another to take an analytical or critical view, and yet another to respond coherently, effectively and developmentally to what the media offers. Christians are constantly assailed by critical views of their faith in the media. They see issues distorted, stereotypes recycled, individuals pilloried, ridicule unanswered, ignorance exalted, and truth despised or arrogantly denied. Usually, at least in Britain, there is little positive reaction from Christians. They are either afraid, unsure how to make their voices heard, divided in their views on substance or tactics, frequently leaderless as regards who effectively speaks for the Churches, or ill-informed on the specifics or technical aspects of the issues being raised.

By reason of their structure and values, religious institutions are in a necessary tension with contemporary media. Cardinal Avery Dulles highlights six points where this tension is most evident: the Church's message is a mystery of faith, whereas the media is investigative and largely iconoclastic; the message of the Church is eternal and seeks to maintain continuity, whereas the media lives off novelty; the Church tries to promote unity whereas the media specialises in conflict; the main work of the Church is spiritual, whereas the media concentrates on more tangible phenomena and selectively reports Church teaching as though the Pope and bishops were mainly interested in sex, politics and power; in a democratic society, the media has great difficulty in appreciating a hierarchical structure and has an inbuilt bias in favour of the disobedient priest and the dissenting theologian; Church teaching is often complex and subtle, whereas the media want stories that are simple and striking.[4]

Even if we acknowledge the spiritual harm that can be done to us personally and culturally by the media, are we not ourselves at least partly to blame? If we see ourselves essentially as victims of the media we do ourselves little justice as intelligent and moral beings. Can we not reposition ourselves, so that instead of being at effect of the media we challenge both the producers and the messages of which we disapprove, those that we discern to be evil or false? This may not be easy for those who have become accustomed to passivity, but that is precisely why we face such issues today. An example of positive response could be the films *Lord of the Rings* and *The Passion of the Christ*. Unlike classic entertainment films of its day such as, for example, *Love Actually*, with its diet of frivolity, licence and satire, *Lord of the Rings* reflects the values of friendship, loyalty, commitment to a chosen task and sacrificial opposition to evil. Similar efforts across a range of media are studied more closely in Chapter 9.

The Catholic Press and television networks are potentially of great importance in making positive use of the mass media. For example, the enterprise of publishing a Catholic newspaper, like that recently initiated in Birmingham, that aims to provide a shop window for the Church, making information and views known on a wide scale and ensuring an alternative to the sceptical, critical, satirical, ironical, postmodern and unbelieving commentary of agnostics and atheists in the mass media, is all part of a work of evangelising culture by its deliberate selection of material, the voice given to the Gospel, its authoritativeness in comment on doctrine, and the development of an ethical viewpoint with respect to contemporary issues.

Bringing gospel values to bear upon secular cultures, affected as they are by rebellion and sin, is itself countercultural. The aim is a purifying or correcting of tendencies that lead humanity away from its destiny revealed in the Gospel. The proclamation of this true destiny is a prophetic work, a God-given challenge, that can perhaps be best explained with an example.

One of the teachings of the Gospel which occasions most consternation is the call to forgive enemies. People find that this is a counsel of perfection and not an option in the modern world. Yes, in small things that do not matter one might be able to put them out of one's mind, but the great human crimes remain unforgivable. Yet Christianity continues to teach that it is precisely the worst crimes, those from which we have most suffered, that we must forgive. The teaching is that unforgiveness locks up our hearts to love, prevents us from continuing to grow as spiritual beings, and blocks the way to holiness. Only the way taken by Jesus, 'Father, forgive them, they know not what they do', can be fruitful in the end. Hearts stuck in resentment, hatred, judgement and other forms of unforgiveness remain frozen until they offer reconciliation. This was a strong teaching of Pope John Paul, and he sought to give an example, not only by apologising for transgressions by the Church in former times to open up the way to forgiveness, or by gathering world religious leaders at Assisi to pray for peace in the world in 2002, but even more at a personal level in forgiving the man who sought to assassinate him in 1981, and in his firm stance against the Iraq war. The work of reconciliation, of peace-making and building the civilisation of love is an evangelising of the culture of the modern world.[5]

NOTES

[1] Pierre Teilhard de Chardin, *Le Milieu Divin*. Paris: Seuil, 1957.

[2] Denis Alexander, *Rebuilding the Matrix: Science and Faith in the 21st Century*. Oxford: Lion Publishing, 2001.

[3] Anthony Rizzi, *The Science Before Science: A Guide to Thinking in the 21st Century*. Bloomington: Authorhouse Press, 2004.

[4] Dermod McCarthy, *Word,* May 2002, pp-7-9

[5] John Paul II, 'No peace without justice, no justice without forgiveness', Message for World Peace Day, 2002.

CHAPTER SEVEN

Awakening Faith

ASED ON THEIR experience and knowledge of the extent to which secular culture has succeeded in marginalising or forgetting God and his revealed truth, Christians see the need for the Church to show the continuing relevance of its faith and doctrine. Such an evangelising approach is not part of the mainstream of human culture, but is instead itself countercultural. That is, the main assumptions, values and institutions of secular culture are called in question by a renewed Christian faith. This does not entail condemnation or rejection of humanity's history and achievements, but rather a re-appraisal of its positive and negative aspects, a purifying or correcting of tendencies that lead humanity away from its true destiny as revealed in the Gospel, and an invitation to people of good will to acknowledge any misunderstandings and prejudices they are bringing with them.

Many of St Paul's Athenian listeners mocked him when he spoke of the resurrection, but a few heard the call of the truth and became believers.

Step four
awakening faith in those who have begun to hear the Gospel preached

The ultimate goal of evangelising people is that 'souls might be lifted up from the world of the senses to the eternal' (LA, 7), so as to bring them to conversion or to renewal of their faith in God's promises. How Christians manage to awaken faith will vary by circumstance and by the creativity and skills of those involved. We know that faith cannot be imposed, and that is not the way of the Gospel in any case. The intent is rather to help people to listen to God, inviting them to open their hearts rather than imposing on them a new view of life, and working especially by example to attract and convert them to wonder, reverence and hope. According to the *General Directory for Catechesis,* in considering God's providential plan of salvation, there are basically three aspects of the catechetical approach that are relevant for us to consider briefly:

a) the 'initial proclamation' of the Revelation of God
Revelation is not only *from* God, but *of* God, and primarily of

Jesus Christ. As Pope Paul VI wrote so succinctly and powerfully, 'There is no true evangelisation if the name, the teaching, the life, the promises, the kingdom and the mystery of Jesus of Nazareth, the Son of God are not proclaimed.' (EN, 22) Therefore all evangelisation refers in the first place to Jesus, to a personal encounter with him (GDC, 53), and to Jesus glorified in the mystery of the Eucharist and in the mystical body of the Church.

b) the spreading of the good news through systematic and comprehensive catechesis
Then comes the message concerning what Jesus has done. He has redeemed us and given us the promise of eternal life if we accept him as Lord. This message is contained in Revelation, that is, in Scripture and in the tradition and teaching of the Church, which in some aspects predate Scripture and have constantly interacted with it (GDC, 44).

c) the definitive call, together with the necessary spiritual formation (GDC, 37).
Whether we are non-believers, lapsed believers, or consider ourselves to be faithful Christians, the spiritual path is one of continuous learning about the faith and of personal conversion and commitment.

This summary does help to get at what is really meant by bringing the Gospel to secular cultures, and provides an introduction to this chapter and the next. All initiatives must begin from recognising where people are, knowing them, getting empathically inside them and their cultures, and drawing them out into a response to hitherto unacknowledged imperatives of care, genuineness, love, service, wisdom and understanding, and everything that constitutes the faith. What needs to be added here is that, in evangelising not only individual persons but also cultures, the evangelist is working for a general spiritual revolution and is encouraging conversion as a cultural movement. If this cultural dimension of the process is achieved there is the hope of reviving a Christian world and renewing the spiritual life of a whole civilisation. Such work requires a new approach and a new spirituality. By its nature it will not be rationalistic and it will not be evolutionary. It will be rather prophetic and revolutionary. It will have to be radical if it is to reverse what has been happening in secular society, and within the Church, for the past three centuries since the Enlightenment.

The inculturation of the Gospel, the making accessible of Christ's message within different cultures (RM, 52), and therefore by different means and in different terms, has existed from the beginning. It is the story of Pentecost. However, the cultural diversification as well as the contrary movement to cultural globalisation that characterise the world in our time are so pronounced that it is now scarcely possible to evangelise by traditional means. The purpose of inculturation is not merely diplomatic, let alone aesthetic; it is to ensure that the Gospel has the maximum possible impact in a specific culture. As an example, inculturation would not mean accepting all the values of a polygamous culture, but rather emphasising those that are consistent with the human dignity of women and the sacramental character of human conjugal love. It is therefore part of a strategy to develop meaningful dialogue in relation to faith, doctrine, morals and the Christian way of life. It opens out into approaches to ecumenism, interreligious contacts and secular ethical and rights issues. Thus, new ways, with a different language and expression, will be found for reaching unbelievers, for example through a new apologetics, one that does not impose or pressurise, but which is based on people's understandings, experience and needs.

Once more we can evoke the potent example of Pope John Paul in the novelty and sheer attractiveness of his ministry in drawing people to listen to the Gospel. The overwhelming confirmation of this has been in the World Youth Days, when so many members of a generation thought to have been lost to faith have hung on to every word from his lips. He challenged the young to respond to the Gospel. More generally, his talks and homilies on the Christian mysteries, even in his addresses to the Roman diplomatic corps and to secular bodies of all kinds, left people in no doubt as to his belief and trust in God not just personally but for the solution to the world's most intractable problems.

Christianity as a countercultural mission

As Christians, do we merely see ourselves in a rivalry with the secular culture, or do we recognise a real power of initiative to seize opportunities for the benefit of our faith and its expression? The concept of culture embraces the Christian notion of person and community, a Trinitarian idea. As was explained earlier, the faith itself is a culture, in the sense that it represents a way of living that diverges from secular cultures. One perhaps sees the point most clearly in those 'primitive' cultures that intermingle secular and sacred aspects, in which religious beliefs are not exculturated. In the West one can say that the culture of Christian faith is virtually separate from the environing secular culture, to the extent that it is coming from an almost distinct value universe, as illustrated by the cultures of life and death which were discussed in Chapter 5. Therefore, Christian culture, the faith, is in effect necessarily a counterculture, one that challenges the prevailing culture in an intention of replacing it entirely, since there can be no long-term co-existence.

A particularly dramatic area of contrasts is that between the Church and the secular mass media. Some sociologists suggest that they are rivals, though in many ways mirror images of one another. They have their own characteristic type of evangelising, attempting to draw people into their distinctive values and lifestyles. Both are seeking to win people's adherence or agreement, and to absorb their time and energies. The media have been accused of holding a monopoly of information and of the cultural agenda. They can decide what is seen and heard. Bourdieu accuses the media of obliging even prominent thinkers to say what they are told, to speak only what is acceptable to producers of programmes. If they do not then they are not given airtime, and that is more than they can endure. So people sell their souls.[1]

The Church and the media thus see the faults of the other rather than their own. So the Church sees the indifference, moral slovenliness, the satirical attacks and half-truths, the fashionable edicts, the secularism and the hypocrisy of the media, and the progressive marginalisation of religion, instead of recognising its own shortcomings. And the media see the arrogance of the Church in imposing its view of reality, its solutions, its attempts to change people's outlooks and behaviour, its conditioning of minds and hearts, the scandals of its failure to live up to its claimed standards, its condemnations of contemporary values and more, instead of recognising its own harshness, hypocrisy and arrogance in the pursuit of its values.

Is there a comparable rivalry between the Church and science? Certainly neither is in a hurry to admit that the other has the more satisfactory explanations of the world. The Church claims expertise in dealing with the why questions, leaving the how questions to the scientist. But it demands humility of scientists for them to acknowledge that their discipline may have reached its limit, that it is better not to speak than to make unsustainable claims about science's understanding of the real, from the meaning and purpose of human life inhering in the soul to the direction of evolution or the source of the imaginative power that has produced the universe. Many scientists make this obeisance, seeing how faith comes to the aid of reason, just as reason can enlighten faith.

And what of young people comparing what the Church and secular culture have to offer them? For most, secular culture affords an initiation into ideological pluralism, which means that they encounter a variety of views or value systems, none of which is allowed to be given preference. Thus everything falls into relativism. There is no truth, no standard of integrity by which they can calibrate their lifestyles with the kinds of moral values or beliefs that concern the Church. While all of us need to find beliefs by which to live our daily lives, these can easily become arbitrary or self-contradictory if there is no worked out foundation for them. Almost despairingly societies look to schools to make up for the moral collapse in the wider society, in order that the young have some models to assist them in developing their own values in life. For those who are mature enough to work things out from experience or with a certain eclecticism, it is already bad enough, because where do they turn for any guarantee of truth, honesty or worthwhileness? But for the young the situation is desperate, because they have little experience and they are often unaware of an alternative to agnostic relativism.

Sadly, it cannot be assumed that Catholicism and Catholic education offer much of a bulwark against relativism. There are too many forces that pull young Catholics away from faith and Christian morality. The most serious is probably the casual disregard for family values that is found almost as much among Catholics as among non-Christians, and often more than among committed Christians of other denominations. The Catholic Church faces a very serious moral and spiritual challenge if it wants to ensure the maintenance of its faith and values in the next generation, and if it wishes to find new priests and have an audible voice in society. Above all it is the young that the Church needs to reach, and to do this it must offer the faith with far more conviction and in radically new ways.

We can in fact find striking examples of initiatives aimed at awakening faith, even if they have not all been universally adopted: street evangelising, courses in initial proclamation of the Gospel, days of renewal, Alpha courses, drug rehabilitation through spiritual means, shelters for the homeless, or pro-life pressure groups, all of which can be undertaken without a strongly proselytising character. They are intended as invitations to people to reconsider where they stand on issues touching on the ultimate meaning and purpose of life.

Evangelising will inevitably involve countercultural ways of dealing with contemporary issues such as education, poverty, discrimination, and respect for human life. Where such problems are under discussion, the Christian response has to be other than the secular. This is because the Christian does not take the problem to himself, but rather entrusts it to God. This does not avoid hard work, but it will rely upon the Holy Spirit. Never has this response been so apt as at the present time when rationalism and science are so confident in their autonomy, a state of mind which according to TPAC 'reveals the sinister contradiction between the affirmation of a will to live and an obstinate rejection of God, the source of all life.' (TPAC , 8)

While the Church does not seek to justify involving itself directly in the political process, it does speak out in those areas which relate to its prime function: the guiding of souls in relation to their spiritual development and eternal salvation. This means that there are times when it appears that there is a Church-State rivalry. We could take the example of the current political situation in Cuba, where there is a government that represses the Church in many ways. The Church does not wish to take over the reins of government, but it has argued strongly with the authorities to secure the freedom to offer the faith to the people, to ensure freedom of worship, and maintain its agencies for the pastoral, educational and spiritual care of its members. The issue that arises is how the Church develops its strategies for moral and spiritual renewal. Is it a question of what society allows, or is it that the Church must stand for its spiritual freedom whatever a particular State decides? Thus in China, should the Catholic Church accept the role of the Patriotic Catholic Church, separated from Rome and subject to the Government, or should it choose to work independently for a spiritual transformation of the whole society in the underground Catholic Church?

Spiritual values - It is noteworthy that the strategies adopted by the modern world to cope with the violent efforts of religious and political fundamentalism, terrorism, nationalism, racialism and war are usually through such means as the arranging of talks, conferences, trade boycotts, and negotiations about the balance of advantages, whereas in fact these responses by rationalists are the measure of their own limitations. The most powerful way to respond to the believer who is regarded as wrong or evil must be by having a stronger belief. It must be in values for values, and in faith for faith, that any solution to the profoundest world crises will lie. If reason pursues its own course separated from faith it becomes lost; it produces monsters like Communism and Nazism. Christian faith, on the other hand, needs to be inculturated, since Jesus became man precisely to show how the truth would set us free, that is, would bring us to the highest expression of our value, meaning and purpose as God's creatures.

So strong has the taboo on the spiritual become in Western secular society, that many erstwhile believers have come to abandon a supernatural faith, and to rationalise their life-stances in cultural and psychological terms alone. Thus reference to the transcendent is hardly tolerated as a part of public discourse, even though it is accepted as ultimate reality by the Church. An important by-product of this peculiarly modern problem is the existence of a form of censorship or persecution in which any manifestations of firm and resolute moral or spiritual conviction are disregarded as intransigent, intolerant or meaningless, or are rejected as irrelevant special pleading, as for example in the case of pro-life arguments over the abortion issue which often attract the jibe that Catholics are merely repeating what the Pope has told them to say.

Despite the mystery of the source and legitimacy of values, or perhaps because of this, values are defended to the utmost, even to the death.[2] While it is unlikely that anyone would voluntarily die for a scientific theory as such, since the matter is there to be conclusively demonstrated eventually, the only way to prove a value is to die for it or, some might argue, to kill for it. Secular society is lost when it comes to trying to understand the strength with which values can be held. Few Westerners really retain the notion of values worth remaining long years in prison for, or dying for, or even of people worth dying for, and thus they could not follow the drift of the Muslim response to the Salmon Rushdie affair. In fact, they have made such a virtue out of tolerance that, when it is put into action, it amounts to a totalitarian constraint on all forms of beliefs in an absolute. However, by their very definition, absolute values cannot be accommodating, and therefore a tolerant, liberal or agnostic society is bound to be perplexed when it encounters them.

If we become convinced of the authenticity of particular values and beliefs, we must hold that these should be lived out, and we must accept the commitment to live them out ourselves. This is not a merely rational process. The step from conviction to commitment is of a spiritual order. Christian teaching shows how this step may be taken, through repentance for past failings, obedience to God's commandments, and the effects of his freely bestowed grace. By looking beyond the relativist understanding of reality, by identifying in faith the ultimate source of values and of truth, it is possible for us to understand, not with the mind alone but with the heart and the soul, the unfailing guidelines and resources of the Gospel and the whole Christian tradition. Faith finds expression in conviction about the good news of Jesus Christ and commitment to following him. These two qualities are essential to any good life. If we waver in our understanding of the good, then we are neither convinced nor faithful. If we acknowledge that our conscience tells us right from wrong, and if we accept the conclusions of our own conscience aided where necessary by external guidance, then it is a matter of will that determines whether we carry through our conclusions into action, and this is commitment.

Secular society uses these words somewhat differently. Conviction is not necessarily positive in meaning, since it can imply unreasonableness, exaggeration, or obsession, and commitment is often attached to such notions as doggedness or stubbornness, as well as to more admirable qualities of perseverance in scholarship or athletic training. Moral conviction and commitment are less often envisaged, or less often prized, since these beg questions about values and beliefs. An example is the contemporary view of marriage in secular society. From commitment 'until death do us part' has evolved a contract that can be revised or abolished according to changed circumstance or intentions. It has been relativised. Commitment is for now, perhaps, but who knows about tomorrow? But for Christians, conviction and commitment remain two essential virtues. Unless they have strong faith they can get nowhere on the path to holiness. They will keep losing the way. It is in this sense that they are saved by faith. However, without commitment too they cannnot carry through the imperatives of faith, the life of holiness, the constantly renewed determination to remain faithful in thought, word and deed, until the end.

From cultural wars to spiritual warfare

Perhaps too many Christians lack a sense of perspective on humanity's journey to God. The evangelising of culture is about seeing the wider picture all the time, and helping others to open their eyes to what is on the horizon. It is less a question of rousing people with warnings or threats than of appealing to them to see what is before their eyes, what has been foretold, what follows from all that they already know in their hearts and consciences, in their experience, and in their culture. This kind of evangelising is for everyone. It stems from dialogue with and articulate responses to the affirmations of secularists, dissenters from Church teaching, denizens of popular culture, celebrities, popular heroes and the false prophets. Is it not staggering to reflect that Frank Sinatra's *My Way* is one of the most popular songs at funerals? Its lyrics are the complete inverse of Christian spirituality.

What this ongoing struggle over basic values between the cultures of secular society and Christianity means for the Church is what some writers have called 'the culture war', in an expression derived from the *Kulturkampf* of 19th century Bismarck Germany. The expression is currently used to refer to the fierce battles of words, ideologies and faiths that have taken place over abortion, gay liberation, religious freedom, hate crimes, sexism, feminism and the Church, child abuse, women priests, the traditional family, sexuality and sexual preference and behaviour, media bias against traditional values and morality, and anti-Christian bias in the media and public life and the courts. It is not that the Church must set out to win such a war at any cost, but that both the Church and every Christian must struggle to gain a hearing for the truth in contemporary life. The great mission of the Church to preach the Gospel to all nations is still there as a command of Jesus, but this mission now requires a prodigious effort of explanation, translation, inculturation and of the evangelising of human culture, if it is to attain its target today in the face of widespread incomprehension and antagonism.

All this is merely an illustration. The point is that the kind of controversy that fuels the culture war is often one that combines moral and religious features, and, especially in the sexual area or linked to the Catholic Church, the Church that is associated in most eyes with traditional teachings and beliefs. Therefore, it is for the Catholic Church and its members to deal with the hard stuff of controversy, and this through both spiritual and cultural means. It is undoubtedly urgent for Christians both to understand what is happening and to be more articulate about their values and beliefs if they are to make them understood more widely, and if they are in any way to counter the allegations, misunderstandings and deliberate misrepresentations of religion by secular media, public authorities, legal and medical opinion, and all those who are ideologically or spiritually motivated to destroy the influence of Christian faith.

It is possible to take up arms in the cultural war with a motive that seems spiritual but which is really ideological or sectarian. The Christian is challenged by Scripture to move from this to an understanding that what is at play is not a worldly conflict but a spiritual warfare, the kind of struggle that St Paul tells us 'is not against enemies of blood and flesh, but against the rulers, against the authorities, against the cosmic powers of this present darkness, against the spiritual forces of evil in the heavenly places' (Eph 6:12). People today are often uncomfortable with the notion of a personal force of evil, despite the fact that Jesus frequently spoke of the devil, and recent popes have done so, including Pope Benedict XVI in the Ratzinger Report:

> ...the devil, as far as Christian belief is concerned, is a puzzling, real personal, and not merely symbolic presence. He is a powerful reality, 'the prince of this world'..., a baneful, superhuman   freedom directed against God's freedom.[3]

People can flatter themselves with a record of cultural campaigning carried out in human strength, but what is going to count in the long run is the battle waged in heavenly strength against evil, by spreading the Gospel rather than by mere debate. What is needed is the spiritual transformation St Paul calls for (Rom 12:2) and the new life in Christ in which minds are renewed through a spiritual revolution. This is an indispensable insight, not so much an added element but a thrust that needs to be maintained. The intellectual gives way to the spiritual, and the spiritual engenders a new identity. This identity is forged not only individually but collectively in a way that helps to transform society and culture, so that humanity as a whole comes to see that the things that really matter are not personal advantage or glory, but knowing the truth, goodness and beauty of God, and being led to the Creator through the things he has made.

Spiritual warfare in religion, life and art – No one can read the Gospels without realising that Jesus saw himself as engaged in a spiritual battle against a personal power of evil. This is shown by his exorcisms, his many references to the devil in his teaching and parables, the story of his temptation in the desert, and his recalling having seen Satan thrown down like lightning from heaven (Luke 10:18). We are most aware that the world is a spiritual battleground when the Church is being attacked, but spiritual warfare affects everyone (Rev 12:17), through family conflicts, wars, ethnic and racial hatred, as well as through dissent within the Church. Believers enter this struggle armed with the weapons of faith and God's grace. In the Lord's Prayer we ask: *lead us not into temptation, but deliver us from evil*. That is, the evil is not of ourselves, but something else from which God can free us. We learn from Scripture that evil is an intelligent and personalised power rebelling against God, using deceit and aiming at the spiritual destruction of human beings.

It can hardly be denied that today we are witnessing total warfare of the spirit, in which the Church is beleaguered in the front line of battle, while its people are constantly being weakened and many are leaving the field, especially in the

West. But it is not a matter of geography so much as of the confrontation between Jesus, who is the truth, and untruth in the form of political oppression, rationalist scepticism, relativism, and hedonism. Can we deny that our personal actions are part of a larger spiritual battle if we buy into consumer culture, enticed by its false promises, greedy for its pretended benefits, or willingly deceived by its lies in advertising, its unethical finances, and its unjustifiable claims on our leisure and personal time? Whatever the peculiarities of particular cultures, this conflict knows no geographical boundaries. It exists in all societies.

A spiritual standpoint enables us to see that the media are involved centrally in the spiritual warfare that is raging in contemporary thought, culture and society.[4] Ineffectually or not, Christians lament that the secular media multiply violence, sexual licence and moral waywardness. An extreme example is the use of the Internet by paedophile rings. Perhaps it is the case that the media have gathered a cadre of people whose morality and ambitions are consistent with an agenda of subjecting society to their own cultural values. It is at least possible that this is a work of evil, every bit as conscious and deliberate as the work of the Church in preaching the Gospel. It is a contrary movement to evangelising. Why are the media so intent on ignoring, or otherwise deconstructing, undermining and rebelling? The answer would seem obvious. This is a work of spiritual warfare.

The issue of abortion is a prime example. Pro-choice advocates accuse those who are pro-life of forgetting the woman, of ignoring the relationship between the woman and the foetus by stressing the rights of the foetus and therefore creating a hostility between the two. This is amazing talk to a Christian, since it seems that the relationship is one of mother and child and that nothing should interfere with this, certainly not by the destruction of one of the lives. It is difficult to understand how this issue survives as a live debate between two positions, when one of them appears so denuded in its special pleading, illogicality and blindness. This can only be ascribed to the spiritual underlay, the profound spiritual warfare that characterises the topic of life and the defence of life. There are Christians who see abortion as a sacrifice that is being offered to Satan from which he derives enormous power over the affairs of the world. Granted this power by our transgressions, the devil can promote sexual degeneration, financial corruption and violent warfare. We have succumbed to the power of the devil by legislating for abortion, and by conniving with the speciousness of the woman's claimed *right* to choose the death of her offspring.

If there is injustice in media comment on religious matters, and still more if there is blasphemy, this must be not simply because of a lack of integrity of the individuals concerned but because of the spiritual warfare that confuses believers and unbelievers alike. Neglecting the spiritual struggle could be either through indifference or malign influence, just as mockery can be mere unkindness or it can be intended to undermine and destroy. A prominent example of media antagonism to religious themes is the treatment given to the film *The Passion of the Christ* by a British TV Channel Four documentary. Mel Gibson was attacked for fundamentalism, egomania, desire for money, astuteness in manipulating the controversy he has aroused, anti-semitism, disloyalty to the Church of Vatican II, sadism ('the Crucifixion according to the Marquis de Sade'), extreme violence that was alleged to have a sexual connotation, reliance upon lurid and paranoid accounts of the passion by Maria Agreda and Catherine Emmerich, and he was said to deserve hell if there were such a place -- and this was all in one programme. There was virtually no opposition voiced to these views. This was hardly an even-handed debate, just a thoroughly evil attempt by a media agency to squash Gibson, to undermine his work, and to dissuade the public from seeing his film.

The Christian needs strong faith and a life of prayer to confront this spiritual warfare. For example, in religion, now as always, there are castes that derive power from being the acknowledged arbiters of religious laws and rituals. A split between clergy and people is the oldest form of spiritual warfare, a corruption engineered by Satan. Similarly, conflicts between different religions and denominations, each claiming God as its own, if not resisted by anxious enquiry and ecumenical efforts, become part of the spiritual war. Other issues such as human rights in freedom of speech and thought, warfare through nationalism or ethnic disputes, and material greed, assume a spiritual character through the divisions between different sets of people acting unjustly, and the rejection of those thirsting for justice and righteousness by those who lack scruples and morality. Finally, in the world of the universities and high culture we see not only the religious and secular conflicts already referred to but also the search for truth being countered by attempts to undermine and corrupt truth and moral goodness by the very power of thought and feeling conveyed through the arts, literature and other works of human imagination.

From this point on we can consider that the diagnosis of the crisis of secular society and culture has been sufficiently explored for it to be obvious what the Gospel demands of the Christian. It is not enough to criticise, however justifiably; nor can it suffice merely to awaken consciences and propose secular solutions. Christians do not possess their faith for the sole purpose of ensuring their own salvation. They are responsible for bringing their faith to others by offering the full revelation of God's teaching and promises to those willing to listen. It is this major work of the passing on of the faith in the midst of secular society, therefore, that will be the ongoing topic of the concluding chapters.

NOTES

[1] Pierre Bourdieu, *On Television and Journalism*. London: Pluto, 1998.

[2] See *Veritatis Splendor's* discussion of martyrdom as 'an affirmation of the inviolability of the moral order'(VS, 90-94).

[3] Josef Ratzinger with Vittorio Messori, *The Ratzinger Report*. Ignatius Press, 1985, p 138.

[4] Nichols, op.cit., pp.43-4.

CHAPTER EIGHT

Teaching and Inspiring Christian Faith and Life

TOO MANY CHRISTIANS have retreated from the public forum where political, social and scientific conclusions are advanced, fearing that they have nothing of value to contribute and that they will only suffer ridicule under the scrutiny of secularists who reject the existence of God. There is therefore a great need for the Church to offer its witness of faith and wisdom to the world of ideas, especially in science, and to form its members to take up the issues that are so drastically affecting humanity at the present in such areas as the rights of the unborn, euthanasia, embryology, population policies, sexual disease control, and indeed in the debates about human self-consciousness, intelligence, and evolution. It is, for example, extraordinary that an eminent scholar can write a book about the human brain and say nothing that is even speculative about consciousness.[1] The existence of human consciousness, however, is not even a problem to the Christian believer who knows, through faith, that the human being is made in the image of God. Once some common ground has been found, or some seeds of the Gospel, the way may be open to a fuller witness. In the Areopagus St Paul seized on the altar to the unknown god, claimed it as prefiguring the God of the Christians, and went on to preach the Gospel in language and ideas borrowed from the Greek culture.

Step five
teaching and inspiring Christian faith and life

While the family is only one of the organisations in society that are responsible for the introduction of new members into the social and cultural world, it is evidently of supreme importance in providing basic learning and role modelling, initiation into social and religious understandings, preparation for social life, for adult roles and responsibilities, for sexuality and for citizenship. Youth peer groups and community influences including church or similar organisations soon come into the picture, but if the groundwork is not laid by the family then social dysfunctions and worse can easily follow. Because there are so many agendas in child-rearing, conflict between the agencies involved is common. The family may be seen as a support or threat by other, often more powerful social institutions, and thus the family is dependent upon the values and attitudes that are held in the wider community. Currently in Western democratic societies the family is in decline because so many either contest the value of the family as traditionally known or consider that alternatives to the traditional family based on Christian assumptions have an equal right to exist. In this situation it is increasingly the case that social and legal frameworks guide and constrain families, or work consciously against traditional patterns out of loyalty to new concepts and values regarding family life.[2]

Apart from its influence through the family on the upbringing of children, the Catholic Church has been one of the world's great providers of formal education and positive moral teaching. Its schooling systems have been one of the ways that it has spread gospel faith and life. The Catholic school has aimed to form and educate people appropriately to their needs and the needs of humanity in general so that they appreciate and assimilate the fulness of Christian doctrine. Often Catholic institutions have been staffed by people who undertook their work as much out of vocational zeal as the need to earn their living. Catholic teachers were also witnesses, even prophets in this sense. Though not all Catholic teachers have taught religion or the faith explicitly, they were engaging with truth, goodness and beauty, and were educating, convincing and forming their students through Christian education, through culture, art, and the whole way of life of the believer. They, and others in allied work of education, catechising and the caring professions, were responding to people's need for spirituality, and revealing spiritual and supernatural dimensions of existence, and thus reinvigorating the truths and values of the Gospel in their cultures. What this suggests in practice is the vital formation role of Catholic institutions of learning and the importance of well ordered teaching, indeed of a new apologetics that can engage with the values, thinking and self-justifications of contemporary cultures.

Spiritual riches of Christian faith

The marginalistion of Christian faith has meant that its spiritual riches are being widely ignored. It is assumed by many non-believers that everything of the faith is a mere historic residue with no contemporary relevance. But even without the eyes of faith an unprejudiced view must see that this is false, and that Christianity, and the Catholic Church in particular, can claim to have made a unique and powerful contribution to the world. This can be seen over a broad panorama of education, caring services, charitable action, the preaching of the gospel message of salvation, ethical reflection, political philosophy, scientific research, and in the formation of coherent societies of well-motivated people able to act in a fully responsible manner at the level of family life, local community, nationally and globally. One of the aims of this chapter is to recall the range, character and state of development of the spiritual resources for evangelisation to be found in the Catholic Church.

Reference is often made to the *institutional* Church, usually in a derogatory way, implying an organisational structure that has somehow drifted away from its original nature, thus becoming an obstacle in the way of true Christian faith. While it is true that the historical Church has had blemishes and has been guilty of injustices and infidelities, these have been acknowledged publicly especially by Pope John Paul who apologised for them and sought to make amends, for example through his numerous initiatives towards the Jews and the setting up of the Galileo Commission. However, it is important not to limit our view to the historical, social, or political aspects of the Church as a social organisation. It is far more than this, and it is vital that the Church's true identity is not discarded on account of such pejorative human interpretations or judgements. What then is this identity, and why is the Church considered by Catholics to be so important?

The Church believes that it has maintained the apostolic succession from the earliest times with all the authority it received from Jesus when he established it under the leadership of Peter (Matthew, 16). Because of its divine origin, the Church is not merely a human entity. It is described by Paul as the Body of Christ, who was both man and God. We need therefore to recognise what the Church really is, apart from the historical and political image reflected in contemporary media. It is not only the public expression of faith in Jesus Christ, the incarnate God, and the continuation of his life, teaching and ministry but it is a sacrament that transcends the earthly and brings the divine into communion with the human. The Church is also the way of life chosen by the holy, in prayer and virtue, and it is the communion of saints, transcending time and space. From the perspective of an individual Christian, the Church is the source of inspiration and the guardian of tradition and doctrine. It is this mystical Church against which the gates of hell can never prevail, and it is because of the divine authority given to the Church that it can teach the revealed truth of God, interpret the Scriptures, and give definitive rulings on doctrinal and moral questions. Indeed, not only can it do these things but it must. That is the duty of the Church.

At this point we are concerned with the role of the Church, and of all Christians, in passing on the authentic teaching of the Gospel to those whose faith has been awakened and who have accepted a Christian identity. These can only be summary points, since they refer to the whole range of activity of the Church over historical time as well as to the future vocation of the Church in bringing the Gospel to all nations. One useful distinction that can perhaps be made at the start to facilitate the task is that between the hierarchical and the charismatic dimensions of the Church that was suggested, though not extensively developed, in *Lumen Gentium:*

> *The Church, which the Spirit guides in the way of all truth and which he unified in communion and in works of ministry, he both equips and directs with hierarchical and charismatic gifts and adorns with his fruits.* (LG, 4)

This distinction broadly corresponds to that in the chapter title between 'teaching' and 'inspiring'. That is, the Church teaches by virtue of its apostolic authority, and it inspires by virtue of its charismatic appropriation of the gifts of the Holy Spirit.

Von Balthasar speaks of the Petrine dimension of the Church, that is its administrative, institutional, and authoritative pastoring aspects, as contrasted with the Johannine dimension of caring, loving, and nurturing, which is characteristic of John and of Mary. This Marian principle of Church order, according to the Catechism, 'precedes the Petrine' (CCC, 773), because it is based upon the holiness of Mary, the one who is so close to the Holy Spirit that, without challenging the Church, she more fully reflects the divine will and more completely intuits the mind of Christ. The hierarchical or Petrine order of the Church is responsible for the ministry of the sacraments by which grace is granted to the Christian. However, it is also understood by the Church that the Spirit is present in each of its members (CCC, 797), and that each one can be inspired for the good of the whole with charismatic gifts.

We thus look to the hierarchical order of the Church for the work of governing the whole body, teaching the revealed faith definitively, catechising and forming Christian believers, determining the application of gospel principles to issues in human life, and representing the Church to the world. It does this through its bishops, its official bodies, and the vast array of its institutions, such as religious orders, schools, universities, hospitals, entities concerned with evangelising, ecumenism, inter-religious dialogue, and other outreach agencies. The charismatic order, on the other hand, as it responds to the Holy Spirit, is the source of prophetic inspiration, of inspired guidance, of virtues and spiritual gifts that challenge the body of the Church to live the Christian life more faithfully and to give an example of holiness for others to follow.

As they are not separable parts of the Church, the hierarchical and charismatic orders together constitute the richness of the Christian faith. To the new believer they offer knowledge of the revelation of the loving and merciful God who calls all into relationship with him and offers the promise of eternal salvation to those who believe. Through the authority of the Church, this infallible teaching is none the less constantly developed and renewed through the Magisterium and the deliberations of the Church councils. At the same time, the Church, under the impulse of the Holy Spirit, functions as a spiritual entity bringing to believers the blessings of the liturgy, the conviction of belonging to the communion of saints, and the power of regeneration and renewal that ensures the vitality of the faith.

The teaching Church - From the moment of Pope John Paul's death there began to be suggestions that he would be given the title 'the Great'. The reasons proposed were diverse, but one element is quite undeniable, and that is the range, depth and coherence of his teaching in the corpus of encyclicals, apostolic letters and exhortations, homilies, catecheses and addresses, in which he touched upon virtually the whole spectrum of Christian faith. It has been said that it will take decades for the Church to digest this teaching, but here I simply want to point out that, while so many clergy and faithful were abandoning the faith, one man could find the resources and strength to proclaim it to the ends of the earth. This must tell us something!

The media are seen by the Church as a tool of immense potential for teaching and for sharing the faith. This is the view repeatedly expressed by the Pontifical Council for Social Communication, and the Pontifical Council for Culture, not to mention Pope John Paul, who never missed an opportunity to encourage the Church to make more positive and discerning use of the media, as on the 40th anniversary of the Vatican Council's document *Inter Mirifica*, when in *The Rapid Development*, he said:

> ... the Church is not only called upon to use the mass
> media to spread the Gospel but, today more than ever, to

integrate the message of salvation into the "new culture"
that these powerful means of communication create and
amplify. (RD, 2)

It would be difficult to improve upon the summary of the tasks that belong to the Church in this field, according to Pope John Paul in his Letter:

In the communications media the Church finds a precious
aid for spreading the Gospel and religious values, for
promoting dialogue, ecumenical and inter-religious
cooperation, and also for defending those solid principles
which are indispensable for building a society which
respects the dignity of the human person and is attentive to
the common good. The Church willingly employs these
media to furnish information about itself and to expand the
boundaries of evangelization, of catechesis and of
formation.... (RD, 7)

There is much to be learnt by Christians from seeing what is involved in the practice of successful communication within the wider society. First of all, there has never been such a range of media, such opportunities for communicators. It is true that some of the ways of communicating, especially through the oratorical arts in preaching and political speeches, have diminished in their importance in Western nations at least because the crowds or congregations are no longer there in large numbers, but new groups of communicators, such as entertainers, teachers in TV documentaries, experts summoned to inform the public, singers and celebrities of stage and screen, therapists, pressure group spokespersons, writers, and so many others, have hugely multiplied. Although much of this communication is mediated by television, and to some extent in written form by newspapers and magazines, novels and non-fictional written work, a great range of qualities of actual communication remain relevant to whatever impact is sought: attractiveness of personality, trustworthiness, articulacy, capacity to reach out to ordinary people, gravitas, ability to amuse and beguile, having a message, consistency, response to market research and other preparatory work, meeting people's expectations, raising people's hopes, bringing something new, carrying conviction, being able to explain things simply, achieving a reputation or renown, doing something different or creative, espousing a cause, delivering results, providing leadership and inspiration. What a world of reflection is entailed for Christians! And yet Pope John Paul brings to the topic an additional dimension. In the final section of the letter, which carries the heading 'To Communicate with the Power of the Holy Spirit', he says:

> *The modern technologies increase to a remarkable extent the speed, quantity and accessibility of communication, but they above all do not favor that delicate exchange which takes place between mind and mind, between heart*

and heart, and which should characterize any
communication at the service of solidarity and love.
(RD, 13)

It should be possible on the basis of current experience of the media and the principles offered by Church teaching to envisage study programmes, training courses, or a whole raft of adult formation initiatives addressing the positive use of the media for the evangelising of culture. What might be some of these potentialities? understanding how to have a voice in the media, from the Internet to correspondence with the Press, and to publishing and the making of videos and other means of communication; the development of confidence in tackling difficult topics and confronting critical or disparaging views, misinformation, confusion and ignorance of the faith; practice of analysis, discussion and writing on controversial issues; better use of the Internet to research topical issues and views in circulation within the Church and amongst those raising opposed ideas and critical voices; knowledge of how to become better informed about Church teachings by the use of Scripture, the *Catechism* and other sources; and finding the voice to respond firmly and promptly with Christian principles and charity. It is a challenge to the Church to find ways to put ideas of this kind into practice.

If it is true that the media reflect people's values, however confused, and respond to the need of their audiences for the

close study of human life, problems, dilemmas, moral
uncertainties, and deep questions of meaning and purpose, it
should be possible to find Christians who can be formed to
discern the valuable and the superficial, the good and the bad,
and thus to open up opportunities for new inputs while
ceasing to be victims of the media. A dramatic example of
this kind of reversal would be the media presentation of the
events of 9/11 in New York: fear and shock at first, then an
attempt to respond in self-defence, the unleashing of anger
and aggression, but also of thoughts of how humanity could
move towards reconciliation and peace. Since that time we
have seen the the evidence of great human qualities shown in
New York, and the moral and spiritual bankruptcy of mere
hostility to terrorists, let alone to Islam generally. A whole
education programme is in process in spite of ourselves.

Jesus as teacher - It is possible to study directly and
fruitfully the way that Jesus taught. Pope John Paul says:

> *The Incarnate Word has left us an example of how to*
> *communicate with the Father and with humanity, whether*
> *in moments of silence and recollection, or in preaching in*
> *every place and in every way. He explains the Scriptures,*
> *expresses himself in parables, dialogues within the*
> *intimacy of the home, speaks in the squares, along the*
> *streets, on the shores of the lake and on the mountaintops.*
> (RD, 5)

What then are the characteristics of Jesus as a teacher? In Jesus we perceive a person who had the strongest possible moral and spiritual commitment, and who was at times prepared to issue commands, but only to his close followers whose loyalty had already been tested, not to the greater public to whom he preached. When he preached it was with authority inhering in what he said, not with the threat of punishment or coercion. His teaching was filled with striking illustrations, images and stories that related to the experience of his listeners, and his own life was an integral part of his teaching. Above all he taught by example, and quite intentionally. As he pointed out after the occasion when he washed the apostles' feet, 'you also should do as I have done to you.' (John, 13: 15)

His attitude to the people he taught was gentle, though he did speak in condemnatory tones to those who refused to listen to his teaching. He approached his audience with care, securing their attention, identifying their need, and challenging their hearts not merely their minds. His parables were more than just moral or precautionary tales. They were illustrations of the moral and spiritual teaching he had to impart which could be understood at many different levels. Thus, a fragment of teaching like the admonition: 'Give back to Caesar what is Caesar's, and to God what is God's' is a teaching about material cares for the listeners who asked, but also about the pre-eminence of spiritual service for those listeners who wanted to learn more. The conclusion is not forced; it is left lying there for motivated individuals to garner.

There is much in the teaching of Jesus that we hardly dare discuss in relation to modern education, social care and pastoral ministry, mainly because we have substituted technique for commitment. Jesus starts from love and belief in the eternal value and destiny of the individuals concerned. He concentrates on essentials. He ignores debates or short-term results, and aims at truth whatever its human cost in effort or sacrifice. No one is manipulated or indoctrinated. No one is ignored, uncared for, or misunderstood. Many of his hearers must have been left pondering his meaning for a long time, perhaps for years. But his words will ultimately have borne fruit because they were words of truth and integrity.

To understand the spiritual dimension of teaching we have to return to the example of Jesus, because there are no adequate theories to guide us, only models of practice. What we can say is that love for the learner and care for their ultimate welfare is the sure guide, and that such love follows from the recognition of each person as created by God in his image. It is in this sense that it is possible to speak in a non-trivial sense of a 'spiritually attuned' teacher. Such a teacher has a holistic view of the learner, and responds to the core of the person as a creature of God. A teacher's knowledge can never be sufficient to justify erasing the individuality of the learner. Jesus always dealt with the whole person with immediacy and love. This came from a life of total self-giving, of prayer, and of a pervasive sense of his divine mission.

Evangelising at the centre of Church life – From the example given by Jesus it is evident that evangelising belongs at the centre of Church life.

> *The seed of evangelisation is sown by those who so closely follow Christ that they are already doing his work. His life is itself a proclamation, and by living it they too become proclaimers of Christ in the Kerygma that prepares the way for others' conversion.* (GDC, 56)

For many Christians their parish is where they assure their devotion to their faith by regular practice, showing faithfulness, building community, extending care, offering worship, collecting alms, and so forth. But what if it was seen that none of these was as essential as evangelising? What would this mean? Christians are not given their faith simply to make sure of their own salvation, but so that they can be an active part of the Church which exists to save all mankind. If they are not evangelising they are not true Church, and there is no true parish.

Can the call to evangelise be met by a specialised group being set up to run courses, or to visit the lapsed, or to catechise the families of those presenting children for baptism? It would not seem so. On the other hand, can we really say that every single person should be an evangeliser? In a real sense I believe we can. This is because all have daily opportunities to evangelise by prayer, proclaiming and sharing their faith, and by the example of their lives. Does that mean that all are doing it anyway, so we should not need to worry about the principle? Again, not so, because we do not win our salvation simply by what we do automatically, unthinkingly, but by what we do to fulfil God's law and to give him glory by mirroring his love. If we are not acting out of love, but simply from habit, we are not exercising our free will to worship and serve him.

There is no future in trying to argue our way out of what this principle means: Christians should seek by all possible means to proclaim God and his good news of salvation, especially to those who do not know him. They may need to be evangelised themselves as part of this process, but they cannot stop at that. Evangelising is an essential element of Church life into which all should be initiated, so that all can make their contribution. If this does not happen, then it is not at all certain that they can be considered faithful Christians. They may simply be there to seek their own advantage, and that means that they risk arriving before the throne of their heavenly judge with their hands empty, for they will have taken what was going for themselves, not as good works to show when God asks them if they have loved their sisters and brothers. This work is of course happening. For example, we can identify in the Church new approaches to catechetics and apologetics, courses in theology for the laity, spiritual initiatives in ecumenism, healing ministries, specialist study centres on medical ethics, organisations concerned with peace and justice, or publishing concerns that give a voice to Christian thinkers. The real issue is whether or not these are widely supported, for that is the call.

Spiritual renewal in the Church

The Church is not a static tradition or lifeless slavery, whatever its detractors believe. The Church of the future will be revolutionary in the spiritual sense. Hopefully before it descends from heaven like a bride, it will be a Church that has forgotten all its inhibitions, prejudices, fears, antagonisms, and the ways it has been obstructing Christian unity, prolonging jealousies and resentments and stifling the Spirit. This is important because, although the Church is needed to save the world, it seems at present as if it is barely tolerated. Worldly powers at best pay it lip-service, while their hearts are far away. The time can be expected to come, however, when the Church will grow to become the model for the life of the world. People will look to the Church to know how to be and how to live. The Church is the memory, the temple of God's Spirit, the Mother and Teacher, and the mediator of the values and truths that come to us from God.

We perhaps sensed something of the potential influence of the Church during the days surrounding the death and funeral of Pope John Paul. The media seemed as it were transfixed by their fascination with the sudden evidence of his global impact, while the faithful and millions of ordinary people stopped to look, and were inevitably confronted by fundamental moral and spiritual issues that the Pontiff's life raised. The question that arose for the Church was whether it could sustain the world's gaze and continue to lead it towards the truth.

The *re-energising* of the Church in culture, of which Nichols speaks in his title, is a multi-dimensional undertaking that is desirable, overdue, and in the context of faith utterly plausible. We see summed up and inter-related in his book a panoply of theology, philosophy, liturgy, Scripture, spirituality and cultural life, all imbued with the divine presence among us of the triune God.[3] There is a complex and challenging discussion of the main threads needed to link these sectors of Christian life emphasising the fundamental contribution of philosophy, the struggle against rationalism and postmodernism, the holding of the line against contemporary relativism, the reconquering of a Christian aesthetic and piety, one which makes special demands upon the witness of the religious and the clergy, but which also challenges the whole Church, the family, local communities, the female sex and the young.

It is interesting to compare Nichols' work with Groeschel's *Reform of Renewal*.[4] Focused on the conversion of the human person, mind, body and emotions, the latter makes patent how vital it is for Catholic Christianity today that the courage to be prophetic and to live differently, counterculturally, the life of Jesus of the Gospels, should find adherents, and begin to form a new generation of the people of God. It is an illustration of the living out of the arguments offered in *Christendom Awake*. We should not neglect our talents, since each is invited to recognise the significance of the particular religious or lay state to which we are called, and through which we are expected by God to do the work he has prepared for us to do. We are however asked to go beyond the individuality of any vocation and to see our particular gifts as intended for the upbuilding of the whole community of the Church. If we accept this, are we not bound to show that we look to God for inspiration and guidance in all that we do, and that we place his concerns first?

To answer questions about our dependence upon God's action and providence we would need to reach a state of honesty with ourselves, of release from addictions to pleasure and to our own security, and from the self-absorption that can blind us to any other reality. And what might that other reality be? The world viewed in the perspective of eternity, humanity made in the image of God, in the Trinitarian unity of love, the hope of eternal life won for us by Jesus on the Cross, but demanding our repentance and change of heart and life. Christians are constantly reminded of these truths, but like others they are solicited by worldliness and can easily fall away from this vision, the vision inherent in the Gospel and always reiterated in the liturgy of the Church. Undoubtedly it is hard for non-believers to recognise that they may not have understood things right, and yet many religious creeds proclaim these realities.

Faith, constantly renewed by prayer and the Word of God, is the only way to the true vision, for it is an interior thing that each must discover for himself. In evangelising we put this vision forward, we seek to persuade, and above all we pray for the conversion of those around us, but it is God who grants the increase through grace. This is a truly spiritual battle, since there are forces ranged against the truth, as there always have been. These forces lull and blind us, and resist our enlightenment, with the conniving of human weakness, false reasoning, addictiveness, selfishness, and the rest. The moral and spiritual conquest of the truth, only possible though God's grace and in the redemptive love of Christ, is the essential task of the Christian, or indeed of any person of good will who is open to the power of the Holy Spirit. At a practical level, then, it is right to continue to work for justice, merciful love, peace and respect for the created world in all the ways that Christian inspiration can devise, but it is necessary to be aware of the hindrances that the devil and ourselves have put in our way, and especially the pride that makes us believe in ourselves, the self-love that makes us put ourselves first, and the sluggishness that makes us postpone our good intentions instead of rushing to implement them, whether in our own moral lives or in the social and political world we share with others.

Yet closer to the heart of the Eucharistic faith of the Catholic is to fully acknowledge the passages of NMI on contemplating the face of Jesus, even though the mystical nature of this papal counsel makes it very demanding. To illustrate this, if I voice the question to someone 'Are you sure I haven't upset you?' it is very unlikely that I am at the same time staring out of the window. Rather I will be looking towards the person concerned, seeking eye contact to be able to know better what they are feeling. This seeking out the interior state of the other is, it seems, what Pope John Paul was writing about, except that it is the relationship with the Lord that is in question, and our search for his presence so that we can be more sure of his love and his mercy. Indeed, the Pope is but echoing the Psalmist: 'Your face, Lord, do I seek' (Ps 27:8).

This translates exactly into our Eucharistic relationship with Jesus. If I sincerely say the prayer at mass: 'Lord, I am not worthy to receive you, say but the word and I shall be healed', once again I cannot be staring into space. I must intend to engage the Lord, to feel the blessing of his gaze upon me, if anything of what I am saying is to be meaningful, including my prayer for healing. It is only, in fact, if I do address these words directly to the Lord, and thus seek his face as I do so, that I can find his love, his peace, his truth, or his forgiveness and the healing that I need. This constant seeking for the Lord, or seeking his face, is prayer. It is the path to holiness through communion with Jesus and through him with the Blessed Trinity.

It is striking that Pope John Paul not only emphasised spiritual priorities for life on earth but singled out holiness as the starting point for all Christians in the building up of the Body of Christ in the Church. It is a radically Christian way of thinking to see holiness as the ultimate criterion for practical decisions:

> *In fact, to place pastoral planning under the heading of holiness is a choice filled with consequences. It implies the conviction that, since Baptism is a true entry into the holiness of God through incorporation into Christ and the indwelling of his Spirit, it would be a contradiction to settle for a life of mediocrity, marked by a minimalist ethic and a shallow religiosity.* (NMI, 31)

We can be intimidated by talk of holiness, and react as if this was not our concern as mere well-meaning but immensely fallible people. Such a project must be for a minority who are especially called. But this reasoning is false, as NMI makes clear by indicating how holiness is not some disembodied state but a grace-provoked process through which all are called to travel in prayer, worship and the service of others. Holiness comes directly from the Holy Spirit, as the Church has always taught, even if this has not always been understood:

> *The great mystical tradition of the Church of both East*
> *and West has much to say in this regard. It shows how*
> *prayer can progress, as a genuine dialogue of love, to the*
> *point of rendering the person wholly possessed by the*
> *divine Beloved, vibrating at the Spirit's touch, resting*
> *filially within the Father's heart. (NMI, 33)*

Spiritual sense and the spiritual dimension of reality – Sometimes the words 'spiritual' and 'holy' are used as if they were interchangeable. This debases them both. The spiritual is a dimension of reality independent of our volition. It is the way things are. God exists and he has created the world to express his will and for his purposes, only some of which can be known to us. The non-materialist aspect of our existence in the world can be ignored, but it cannot be abolished. Holiness is something quite different. This does depend upon our volition in the sense that although we cannot make ourselves holy we most certainly can prevent ourselves from becoming holy. God has willed a process by which the rational beings he has created can fulfil a destiny to become more like him, united with him, fulfilled by him, in freedom but with his assistance. A fuller exposition of this point would of course need to speak of the incarnate and glorified Christ as Head of his Body through whom the sacramental and communal life of the Church forges a new cultural identity as a sign and instrument of a spiritually renewed society. The key point is that holiness, to which all are called, is humanity's effort of will aided by God's grace to return to its source in God. This renewal of humanity is the business of religion; it is the purpose of Christ's life on earth; and the Church teaches that it is the primary meaning and purpose of human existence.

Often claims are made in secular culture to a kind of intuitive spiritual sense that is independent of the idea of a God. People suggest that high levels of aesthetic and artistic sensitivity, or philosophical questioning of meanings and purposes in life, are examples of a kind of secular spirituality. The proposal that such attributes of the human mind are equivalent to spirituality in the sense of awareness of a transcendent God is of course inadmissible, but we need to keep this secular claim in mind. There are also those, for example in New Age-based religions, who, while not believing in a personal God or even while being agnostic in this regard, do understand there to be a power that transcends the individual, a force that unites people, that gives them a significance or a purpose beyond themselves, and this leads to a type of spiritual sense that may well be non-materialistic and in many ways beneficent.

Christians can respect such beliefs, even while finding them inadequate. Does such a force exist independently of human beings? If so, then how does it differ from the Divine Being accepted by major world religions? If it does not exist independently of human beings, then how did it come into existence? If it was simply a feature of the natural world or the human imagination, how has it happened that there are human beings who are capable of transcendent emotional and spiritual understandings and acts, such as those of love and sacrifice? The Christian answer to this is clear: human attributes mirror those of God, in whose image and likeness human beings have been made. We *descend* from a transcendent God who created inanimate and animate nature and humanity; we have not *ascended* from a god or power that would be inexplicably immanent in nature. It is this awareness of, and faith in the transcendent God, thus recognising a spiritual dimension to reality that stems from and depends upon God, that distinguishes the Christian not only from the materialist, but from the believer in pagan spiritualities.

Evangelising youth culture – The activities of new movements, orders and communities under the impulse of the Holy Spirit are an obvious example of the riches of the Church, especially in the way that their evangelising work reaches subcultures which might have been thought to be least accessible to Christian faith, such as those of youth, drug-addicts and hedonists, or New Age groups. A recent study of young Christians in the United States focused upon converts to orthodox faith among both Catholics and Protestant denominations.[5] Janice Connell reports revival and renewal that is much more observable among the young than the parental generation. The 'new faithful' are mainly young people who are coming to Christian faith without a religious background. They are often highly gifted individuals, frequently having already achieved early goals in their secular careers, but finding things wanting. In a series of 500 interviews Connell identifies a rebellion of the children of the baby-boomers, those who deserted the Church in the 1960s mainly for moral reasons. This movement is largely occurring on campuses, but extends to some of the new ecclesial movements. They are young people who enter secular professions in which they hope to spread the Gospel by taking issue with the degenerate culture of moral relativism and hedonism. It is their grandparents who welcome this new faithfulness while, Connell reports, the parental generation reacts negatively.

Britain is at a different stage. The same phenomena are evident, but on a reduced scale.[6] The problems of the Church in Britain need tackling through evangelising the baptised, catechesis of parish leaders, development of new movements and the formation of leaders with sound doctrine and prophetic vision in these movements. Added to this, there is a need for support from Church leaders who themselves often appear confused and fearful, or even concerned with other agendas. The wider cultural context is that described in the *General Directory of Catechesis*: the loss of faith and a sense of sin, and a confused search for the spiritual. This is a culture that is hostile to institutional religion, fearful of fundamentalism, ignorant of the Gospel, and yet so seductive for young people in its gratifications and false promises. We should therefore be encouraged by the signs of renewal that we see especially in the US, in France, Germany, Italy, Spain and Poland. The new movements among the young are an essential part of this. But we see also that many young Christians lack a strong intellectual and doctrinal basis to their faith. A formation programme alone will not transform such individuals, but it can make a contribution by helping to build a more coherent vision of the faith based upon Scripture, tradition and Church teaching in a contemporary post-Vatican II setting. And in fact the programme for this is surely that which is offered in NMI: spirituality, formation and involvement in the new evangelisation, and which is being developed in centres like the Maryvale Institute in Birmingham.

What can young Catholic Christians do when challenged to choose whether to be loyal to their faith or their culture? The gap is enormous. The Church hardly seems to understand their needs and interests. It takes a prophetic leap on the part of any individual young Christian to attend a World Youth Day or a Youth 2000 retreat, or to join a new community in which a reconciliation of faith and the modern world might be possible, where modern technology, communications, travel, art forms and types of work can be rendered faithful to the Gospel. For most, the join is too difficult to make, and thus they do not try. They drift away from practice of the faith and begin to stereotype it like the rest of their generation. Has the older generation failed them by resolutely refusing to understand who they were and what they needed, perhaps because it stereotyped them too?

It is surely reasonable to argue, first, that young people have a human right to engage with spiritual insights and to encounter what some believe to be the highest sources of meaning and purpose in life. Secondly, young people need to work out their own values and viewpoints, and to select their own lifestyles, but only as a result of considering genuine alternatives. And thirdly, we have to recognise that many young people have a real desire to engage in a practical search for the worthwhile, and this must involve a journey of discovery carried out in freedom. Over against such rights, it seems self-evident that parents, teachers and other helpers have a responsibility not to abandon the young, as has happened so much in the last couple of generations, but to give them every support and encouragement, as Pope John Paul requested when he described the Jubilee 2000 as 'an event of grace... poured out on the Church.' He especially called attention to the participation of young people in the Jubilee, chiding the Church for its pessimism about the young: 'the young have shown themselves to be for Rome and for the Church a special gift of the Spirit of God.' (NMI, 9)

Charismatic gifts – Our communication with God, which we call prayer, flows from the understanding of our relationship with him. Prayer is the deliberate communion we have with God, whatever its precise form, and it is important for developing that relationship, by expressing our love, gratitude and worship, and for drawing down upon us and our world the blessings that God desires to give. We open our hearts to the sanctifying Spirit in the dialogue of prayer. Pope John Paul II believed that, despite the secularisation of today's world, there is 'a widespread demand for spirituality' (NMI, 33). Through the liturgy, especially the Eucharist, we encounter Christ as the unifying force of our bond with God and each other. In the sacraments we find mercy and grace both for the individual and for the Church to defeat sin and evil. Other gifts of the Spirit which also need fostering in Catholic life must surely include prayer ministry, healing, deliverance and prophecy.

Scripture and culture – A scriptural faith would necessarily be critical of any specific culture, and this was in part the explanation for the strong motivation of some of the Reformers. However, Catholics are increasingly devoted to the Scriptures and one wonders what purification might be expected from this. Scripture is the living Word of God, that is to say, what God intended for the world, for humanity and for the Church. In some way it was foreseen that mankind would mould culture around the divine principles to be discerned in the Scriptures. Respect for the Creator, for life, and for nature, obedience to the commandments, peace and order on earth, are seen as the pathway to eternity, and morality is the appropriate response to God's Fatherhood and the way to salvation. The biblical vision of the world along such lines has been obscured if not erased by human history. The rediscovery of the Bible is one means to a purification of the world. God's Word stands as the signpost for human society, the way, the truth and the life. Whatever philosophies and sciences we resort to in order to find a guide for our lives, it is the Bible that offers us the fundamental values and truths which cannot be escaped. Contemporary culture is in a blind alley because it has abandoned the biblical route map.

Marian spirituality – Catholic and Orthodox Christians accept as natural an openness to Mary as their mother and as the Spouse of the Holy Spirit, and they accept her call to obey God, to 'do whatever he tells you' and the model that her life and submission to the Spirit provide. Knowing Mary as mother and intercessor is especially characteristic of the Catholic Christian. The great tradition of prayer to and through Mary is a vast resource of the Catholic Church, as can be seen from the cathedrals and shrines dedicated to her all over the world, the pilgrimages, special prayers such as the rosary, her liturgical feasts, and the many spiritual devotions that have been a feature of Catholic life since time immemorial. In calling the Blessed Virgin the 'Star of Evangelisation' guiding the whole Church to the Lord (TMA, 59), Pope John Paul associated her with a new Advent of faith. This is a theme to which he frequently referred, as when in the exhortation following the Synod of Bishops for the Americas in 1999 he evoked the role of the Blessed Virgin in a most graphic manner:

> *In America, the mestiza face of the Virgin of Guadalupe was from the start a symbol of the inculturation of the Gospel, of which she has been the lodestar and the guide. Through her powerful intercession, the Gospel will penetrate the hearts of the men and women of America and permeate their cultures, transforming them from within.* (*Ecclesia in America*, 70)

Invitation to a loving relationship with God

What all these riches of the spiritual life lead to is the greater recognition and development of the Christian's relationship with God. Through faith in his existence and the belief that he wants us to exist eternally in his company, Christians are invited to look beyond mortal life towards the consummation of a loving spiritual union with God. Already the internal voice of conscience shows us that there is a difference between good and evil, that good is superior, and that a life lived with respect for the good is more worth living, but Christianity also promises a reward for the sacrifices made for the sake of integrity. Christian faith guides the believer to the source of wisdom. Can we deny the right of Jesus to be heard when he both lived such a manifestly good life and claimed that this was because he came from God to teach the truth and the way to eternal life? Surely only a small opening of goodwill would ensure that someone would take such an approach seriously, and that to rubbish it as incredible or too demanding before considering it would be to manifest a self-evidently deficient moral, spiritual and even human sense? As far as the Christian is concerned all the spiritual resources of faith are never to be regarded as personal possessions or privileges; they exist to bring all people to God, and therefore are to be constantly deployed in the evangelising of people and of cultures.

NOTES

[1]Susan Greenfield, *The Human Brain*. London: Weidenfeld and Nicolson, 1997.
[2]Lynette Burrows, *The Fight for the Family*. Oxford: Family Education Trust, 1998.
[3]Nichols, op.cit.
[4]Benedict Groeschel CFR, *Reform of Renewal*. San Francisco: Ignatius Press,1990.
[5]Janice Connell, *The New Faithful: Why Young Adults are embracing Christian Orthodoxy*. Chicago: Loyola Press, 2002.
[6]A similar gathering up of conversion testimonies of several young people has been published in Britain. See Tara Holmes, *Changed: Stories of God's Power to Change Lives*. Stoke on Trent: Alive Publishing, 2005.

CHAPTER NINE

Creating Beauty

WHILE THE VERY notion of truth can appear oppressive in a postmodern culture that has rejected absolutes, beauty retains its power to evangelise, mainly because beauty has the potential to engage and convince and can often speak more powerfully and pervasively in the human spirit. Beauty opens our hearts to the divine, and the divine opens our hearts even more than our minds to beauty. As Pope Benedict XVI said:

Being struck and overcome by the beauty of Christ is a more real, more profound knowledge than mere rational deduction. Of course we must not underrate the importance of theological reflection, of exact and precise theological thought; it remains absolutely necessary. But to move from

here to disdain or to reject the impact produced by the
response of the heart in the encounter with beauty as a
true form of knowledge would impoverish us and dry up
our faith and our theology. We must rediscover this form
of knowledge; it is a pressing need of our time.[1]

This opens up some significant questions for us. What is our concept of beauty? Is it something subjective, something that can be created by human beings, or is it something that intrinsically reflects the divine? Where do I find beauty in my existence and awareness? And do I make up my mind on my own, do I trust an intuition, or are there criteria of beauty that I can adopt? What if we could even see evangelising culture as a revealing of beauty as much as of doctrinal or moral truths? Philosophically, of course, these three, beauty, truth and goodness, belong together, but there is no reason why one of them should not be a distinct focus. In this chapter I concentrate on beauty, not to the exclusion of truth and goodness, but because I believe there is a valuable insight into how modern minds might most easily approach the transcendent. In terms of the argument of the book, however, and the sequence of the seven steps to the evangelising of culture, we need to reflect upon beauty not only in itself, but in its inter-relationship with truth and goodness. We can see this subtle evoking of God's true nature in the words of St Paul in the Areopagus: 'Since we are God's offspring we ought not to think that the deity is like gold, or silver, or stone, an image formed by the art and imagination of mortals.' (Acts: 17:29)

Step six
discovering ways in which inspired human imagination can, by creating beauty, help to bring gospel values to bear in society and culture

The search is for how to infuse culture with faith, to foster the good we find in it, to give expression to beauty and truth that can enlighten, liberate and sanctify people, and transform and redeem culture. In his extraordinarily personal and penetrating letter written to artists, Pope John Paul suggested that by seeking out and revealing God's beauty, truth and goodness in nature and in human creation, and by finding our creative inspiration in God, we can make art and culture bridges to religious experience (LA, 10) and to knowledge of God. By creating media and other realisations that evoke and glorify God we seek to participate in his creative work.

We might think of illustrating the good, the beautiful and the true by reference to human culture, so that the evangelising of culture would be the specific work of creative artists and others inspired by the Holy Spirit, who were able to bring out of the works of culture a meaning and value that were transcendent. However, it is not only artists, but many simply exercising their normal responsibilities in society who contribute to human welfare, culture, science, politics and the environment in ways that reflect God's transcendent qualities. The critical issue then becomes, given the gap between Christian faith and postmodern culture, a seeming dearth of contemporary Catholic literature, art, music, and a muting of Christian principles and values in ethics, science, politics, family life and human relationships, what response can we make, as creative work, critical awareness or spiritual renewal? It must be true that Christian education, proclamation, catechesis, as well as all intellectual work motivated by the Gospel, are contributions to the reconciliation of faith and culture. However, the project goes beyond this, since it is for Christians to contribute to the development of culture through original intellectual work, the development of just laws and government, works of discovery and invention, creative art, new forms of spiritual engagement, social solidarity, entertainment and myriad other ways in which human vision can be extended to encompass more of God's creation and plan.

Truth, goodness and beauty: the ultimate criteria for culture

Some may think that truth, goodness and beauty are three positive aspects, and that one can arbitrarily select which to emphasise, or that one or other of them is not relevant or important for a particular work. However, the secular way of viewing truth, goodness and beauty is quite distinct from that of the believer. These are attributes of God, who is the absolute standard for them. Moreover, they form a trio that interact, just as the three persons of the Trinity interact and belong together as one. This was the way that the so-called 'transcendentals' were seen by theologians from the middle ages to modern times.[2] These absolutes can be identified in the created works of God, in nature and especially in the spiritual nature of humanity, as a divine reflection. And they are also found in the creative works of human beings, mirroring God, however imperfectly.[3] The transcendentals are those things that pertain to God, that are intimations of the Most High, not mere human creations. We may see them at first as things we have thought or made, but then we have to recognise their true authorship. Just as in nature we perceive the awesome beauty of God, so in human works we find the inspiration and instrumentality with which we are gifted by God. It could even be said that the unity of these transcendental qualities becomes the arbiter or criterion of the degree of perfection to be found in creation and in human culture. This is because so much of contemporary culture rejects the very notion of truth, confuses goodness and evil, and offers only a pretence of beauty.

The *truth* identified with the person and teaching of Jesus transforms our vision of intellectual life, enquiry, science, media, culture and the reality of the world. It leads to belief in a transcendent God, and in the existence of an absolute even where we cannot seize it or where we can only dimly apprehend it. But there is a common modern aversion to truth, a sense of our inability to know anything for sure, or the conviction that a fact was always an interpretation. Many are postmoderns without knowing it, practising the tactic to achieve power over others by pulling the rug of trust and certainty from under them. This leads to a condescending attitude to religion; not dismissing it entirely, but not wanting to be ensnared by it, still less to give it any personal commitment.

Goodness cannot be a stratagem used by people to manipulate reality, subjectively or in the eyes of others. It is the reflection of God in his creation, and it is an option open to creatures gifted with free will, though only through grace. The goodness of the apparently most obscure people may be the most important, the good of the humble rather than the good that brings worldly honours, the gratuitous good that most nearly mirrors the goodness of the Creator. Equally, though, the postmodern mind is sceptical or suspicious about the idea of goodness, or about recognising the good in others, and disabused about the attractiveness of the good. Such people can be unreachable by the good, and more interested in finding out what was a person's unique viewpoint or motivation for action. The belief that there is no morality at all, other than as determined by the subjective feeling of individuals, means that moral relativism and narcissistic individualism are unchecked. The anarchic consequences of this collapse is perhaps most clearly seen in the lack of moorings shown by the young in the revolt against parents and teachers from an early age, increasing lawlessness in the teen years, and the lack of stable lifestyles in later life, especially among those most failed by their parents through broken marriages, violence and sexual abuse.

As for *Beauty*, it is not a matter of taste, education, civilisation or culture. It is rather the attribute of fittingness, the appearance and style of what is good, true and desirable. This helps us to recognise the false beauty of the thing that is merely imitative, superficial, or deceptive, what Scruton refers to as *kitsch*.[4] Beauty can be simple, minimal, innocent of refinements, or it can be rich, overpowering and transcendent. But the essential quality is that it is authentic. It is pure. It is transparent rather than overlaid. It invites to contemplation and hints at the beyond. It cannot be possessed, but offers a pathway towards its own source. However, there is also a corrupted vision of beauty, subordinated to our needs, a consumer-led version. Some of this enjoyment of beauty, when it is not entirely selfish, is mere political correctness, following of fashion, or having the appropriate standards for one's social group. Natural beauty is treated as something to be consumed rather than to be awed by, possessed rather than revered.

In reflecting upon the character of created beauty we can take the cul-de-sac quality of contemporary culture almost as a starting point. As Chiara Lubich puts it,

A sceptical and cold rationality, dealing with things without penetrating them to their original depth, has

replaced the loving understanding that was capable,
rather, of grasping the truth and beauty of creation at its
roots, that is, in God who contains creation within himself
and nurtures it with himself.[5]

Yet now in the aesthetic realm, intellectuals have turned away even from rationality, let alone from any ultimate reality or any definitive criteria of excellence, and have instead chosen the profound relativism of postmodernism. Such reliance upon the individualistic perspective has brought about fragmentation of the whole project of the arts, whether in literature, the plastic arts or the media, so that no one can claim criteria of excellence or superiority. Beauty is now solely in the eye of the beholder. Such a spiritually indiscriminate and limited understanding of beauty can lead us to despair. Pope Benedict described it thus:

A beauty that is deceptive and false, a dazzling beauty that
does not bring human beings out of themselves to open
them to the ecstasy of rising to the heights, but indeed
locks them entirely into themselves. Such beauty does not
reawaken a longing for the Ineffable... but instead stirs up
the desire, the will for power, possession and pleasure.[6]

The relationship between the transcendentals is succinctly portrayed in the Catechism:

The practice of goodness is accompanied by spontaneous
spiritual joy and moral beauty. Likewise, truth carries

with it the joy and splendour of spiritual beauty. Truth is beautiful in itself. (CCC, 2500)

A parallel thought occurs in Scruton's work, when he says that 'it is in our feeling for beauty that the content, and even the truth, of religious doctrine is strangely and untranslatably intimated to us.'[7] The transcendentals belong as one. Separated, they can become idols, no longer reflective of God but instead of human pride, rebellion and self-worship,[8] and this is what we find in secular culture, in justifications for false beauty, in false enquiry into truth, and in evil masquerading as goodness.

The danger is that all criteria for artistic judgement are collapsing into a postmodern morass, and the world of culture is once more especially in need of lasting standards of truth and beauty capable of outliving the innovators of the day. Many contemporary works of art, for example those of Tracey Emin and Damien Hirst, appear to be designed to shock rather than to inspire. One of the least fortunate aspects of contemporary cultural disarray is the rise of the conviction that there are no artistic standards, and that the merely popular has entitlement to as much respect as the work that has survived from one age to another. The grossness of this cultural decay is well described by Scruton, but he is far from noting all the dangers, the failure of the education system to form the young to any consistent criteria of taste, the brashness of contemporary design in the environment, the unacceptability of mere shock as a substitute for artistic development, the loss of roots for popular culture as much as for high culture, and the meaninglessness of so many cultural pursuits as if they could be their own justification without reference to the history of ideas and values. The test for the authenticity of culture must be its integrity, its wholeness, and indeed the way that these attributes combine and enhance each other is the evidence for their integrity. This wholeness is not always realised, even where the intent to find the absolute is present, because of man's fallibility and moral weakness. But we can identify a range of works in terms of their spiritual integrity, from those, like Emin's or Hirst's that, whatever their technical qualities, are self-referring or even degenerate, to those in which the spiritual dimension is implicit, as in the sculpture of Barbara Hepworth or of Antony Gormley in the *Angel of the North* or his figure of a standing man *Sound II* in the crypt of Winchester Cathedral, to those in which the intent to find the Absolute is overpowering, as in icon painting or the architecture of Antoni Gaudi. In other words, not everyone is equally gifted with a sense of the transcendent. Matisse is reported to have said, in answer to a question about his beliefs, that he was a believer only when he worked. Anyone who has experienced the spiritual impact of his Chapel of the Rosary in St Paul de Vence will sense the tantalising quality of this remark.

The critical effort to recognise and bring forth the spiritual dimension to be found across such a range of work is in itself redemptive, as many who appreciated Sr Wendy Beckett's success in drawing spiritual meanings out of paintings in her television programmes must acknowledge. The search for seeds of the Gospel's truth in culture, the bringing to light of elements of goodness and beauty, their clarification, showing forth their radiance, harmony and integrity, their completion through positive criticism and appreciation, through the encouragement of the artist, and the linking of elements of culture to the spiritual life and to God, are all part of the process of spiritually regenerating culture. Christian artists and writers, leaders and pastors are all aware of the suspense involved in sowing the gospel seed, and then waiting. How can the harvest be encouraged? What words, actions, works, commentaries or questions can provoke fruitful reflection? What roadmaps, suggestions, signposts or reassurances can help searching hearts and minds to find peace in faith? This work is the evangelising of culture, the marking out of trails that provide links between culture and faith, between the deep roots of transcendent reality and the cultural strivings of the people of a particular age to formulate what to them seems quintessentially important, even prescinding from belief in God.

Beauty and faith

The deep appreciation Pope John Paul showed for human creative work found expression not only in his teaching and such documents as his *Letter to Artists*, but also in his own life and his personal writings. It cannot I think be an exaggeration to say that his life was itself a work of beauty, as judged by the major biographies, by his own fictional works, poetry and his autobiographical works. As one example one could take his book *Rise, let us be on our Way*, a work written towards the end of his life in which he reflects on his experiences as a bishop, and in which one finds an intensely moving story as well as an extraordinary coherence of spirituality and faith in God.

Michael Mayne, in a differing approach, suggests how the arts, theatre, painting, architecture, poetry and especially music, all have the potential to arouse the spiritual sense.[9] However, I am doubtful about Mayne's breadth of view of the spiritual, because he allows many kinds of inspiration, creativity, sensitivity, insight, feeling and so forth as spirituality, and yet he is a believer and would know the difference between something that is self-referred and something that is from God. He is perhaps too much in love with art per se, and could lead us to run the risk of missing the transcendent altogether. Art is not spirituality. Those that see art as an end in itself are stripping it of its true significance, which is that it is the human giftedness from God that allows such expression. We are not autonomous; all truth, goodness and beauty have their origin in God. The transcendentals are never mere human creations. We may see them at first as things we have thought or made, but then we have to recognise their authorship, just as in nature we perceive the awesome beauty of God, so we find in human works the inspiration and instrumentality that originates with God. This is why Mayne's reference to 'secular spirituality' is misleading. If the human being has an 'inner journey', desires to research 'meaning and purpose', and has a spirit that is hungry for goodness, beauty and truth, that is because, in Augustine's famous reflection, his heart is restless until it finds its rest in God.

Mayne's view of the arts as born of contemplation and stillness, wonder and mystery, is attractive, but again misleading if separated from God, as when he speaks of art nurturing the spirit. This personification of art is reification. The true source is the Holy Spirit in us. What is the numinous of which Mayne speaks, if not God? If Shakespeare is capable of presenting the numinous, what is it to which this refers? Art shows the imprint of God on his creation. A powerful related idea is that beauty and art are incarnational, but this directly refers to God. Mayne points out that artists, painters or novelists work on very ordinary things, such as light, love, nature and objects, but they use them to go beyond, through wonder, to the mystery. But there is a risk in our world that art usurps the role of religion. For example, music can be exalted to the point where it becomes a kind of symbolic theology, bringing order out of chaos, or therapy for disturbed people, as in the reputed 'Mozart effect' with hyperactive children. If so, then it is for believers to reassert the place of art as revelatory of God, and never as a substitute for the transcendent.

This 'incarnational' dimension of art was also part of the message of Pope John Paul II, when he called attention to the sacred character of creative work and referred to the artist as the 'image of God the Creator', reminding him that 'With loving regard, the divine Artist passes on to the human artist a spark of his own surpassing wisdom, calling him to share in his creative power.' (LA, 1) The good and the beautiful are connected, because art has both a moral and productive aspect, and beauty 'is the visible form of the good'. And the truth is similarly connected: 'It is in living and acting that man establishes his relationship with being, with the truth and with the good.' (LA, 2) What is remarkable about the Pope's *Letter* is that in it he defers not at all to the human glories of art, sculpture and architecture. Instead, he returns to their ultimate source of inspiration in the Incarnation:

What has characterized sacred art more and more, under the impulse of Humanism and the Renaissance, and then of successive cultural and scientific trends, is a growing interest in everything human, in the world, and in the reality of history. In itself, such a concern is not at all a danger for Christian faith, centred on the mystery of the Incarnation and therefore on God's valuing of the human being.' (LA, 9)

How can particular forms of beauty be made part of the Christian message? The whole world of art, literature, music and intellectual culture constantly provides insights into truth, goodness and beauty that can be recognised as traces of the transcendent; the lives of many people devoted to others and to causes that demand sacrifice, generosity and love, can be seen as intimations of godliness; the world of intellectual endeavour, knowledge and research in science especially, but in virtually all disciplines, can be regarded either as part of an effort to prove the non-existence of God, or as a persistent reminder that everything we discover has been put there by a supreme intelligence capable of rejoicing at our following his trail. A sampling of such contributions to the evangelising of culture by artists and writers may help to make the point clear that it is not art undertaking some kind of forced labour but art being the best and highest reflection of the true, the beautiful and the good that effectively bears the strongest witness to the Creator. The following are one person's selection, but are intended to encourage readers to think in this way about those areas of the creative arts that they find most inspiring.

Beauty and the creative arts - In writing about the work of Fra Angelico, Saward expresses very cogently the way that beauty, goodness and truth are multiplied in their power by being united. This perhaps becomes clearer if we compare the work of Fra Angelico and Picasso. The latter is certainly a consummate artist. *Guernica* or the *Demoiselles d'Avignon* are extraordinary achievements of human artistry. However, that is also their limitation. To interpret these works in their value for humanity we would need to see that cubism was an experiment of its time, an exaggeration to make a point, an idea taken to its logical extreme. This work is not a synthesis of truth, goodness and beauty, even though it may have some elements of each of these in its ideas, moral outrage, colour and so forth. It says nothing about eternity, infinity, love and glory which are of the essence of Fra Angelico's paintings. Many artists in fact recorded their vices in paint. They offered their rebellion, pride, cynicism, mockery, corruption, even mental illness. We marvel at the beauty coming out of ugliness, but this is a dark beauty, one without the integrity of morality. It is a mere cri de coeur, an essentially inarticulate longing tinged with despair, desperately in need of truth and conversion of heart.

A remarkable exhibition of paintings and sculptures called *Seeing Salvation* was held at the London National Gallery to mark the Millennium. It took its title from the words of Simeon, spoken in Luke, when he beheld the infant Jesus 'Now let your servant depart in peace, for I have seen the salvation prepared for your people Israel'. The exhibition portrayed the impact in Western art of the life of Christ, showing how art is able to reflect on the meaning of life, suffering, death and resurrection, and the place of wisdom and virtue as choices open to humanity in its freedom. The paintings and sculptures shown were being made available through an entirely secular channel, and to a conventional gallery-going public, but with the unexpected result that it became the most successful event of the Millennial celebrations in the UK. People have described visitors to the exhibition as behaving in ways that are very unusual for such crowds. Queuing for admission and packed closely together in the exhibition rooms they were respectful, reverent, explaining things to each other. One of the organisers of the exhibition summarised the surprising public reaction:

> ...the response to the exhibition and the religious images in it was profound and thoughtful and recognised the role that images can play in making the mysteries of Christianity visible, in calling people to faith and deepening believers' experience of it.[10]

Such an exhibition illustrates how seeds of the Gospel can be taken up and planted to grow in a new soil where they could once more, in the power of the Spirit, become a stimulus to pondering vital questions about life and faith. Pope Benedict XVI proposes a way to truth through the beauty of art, especially the art of the icon and the portrayal of Jesus Christ and the saints:

> To admire the icons, and the great masterpieces of Christian art in general, leads us on an inner way, a way of overcoming ourselves; thus in this purification of vision

that is a purification of the heart, it reveals the beautiful to us, or at least a ray of it. In this way we are brought into contact with the power of the truth. I have often affirmed my conviction that the true apology of Christian faith, the most convincing demonstration of its truth against every denial, are the saints, and the beauty that the faith has generated. Today, for faith to grow, we must lead ourselves and the persons we meet to encounter the saints and to enter into contact with the Beautiful.[11]

Transcendence and the written word – Just as we need not realise that we evangelise a person when we influence their attitude to the faith by something we do or say, so it is not necessary for the evangelising of culture to be explicit or deliberate. This is important if we want to be able to understand how the work of Christians as artists, politicians, or parents, for example, can achieve tasks in the building of God's Kingdom simply through sincerity, faithfulness and good will. This question arose for me in reading Ian Ker's book, in which he suggests that there has been a Catholic literature from the mid-19th to mid-20th centuries which amply refutes Cardinal Newman's view that English literature was Protestant and nothing could be done to change the situation. The works of Catholics did not meet the standards of classics, but were ephemeral and would not outlast their authors' lives.[12] Ker's discussion of the work of Graham Greene and Evelyn Waugh is of special interest. He acknowledges both authors as of considerable literary standing, but points out that Greene exhibits only a limited Catholic phase of writing that produced four books, albeit his masterpiece *The Power and the Glory*. Greene's special interest in the theology of sin and redemption evidently intrigued his readers and provided them with insights into the faith, but it was not sustained, and so some of the evangelising influence he may have had was subsequently undermined by his well-publicised negative judgements and doubts about Catholic orthodoxy. Waugh, on the other hand, always kept his interest in the down-to-earth realism of the lived Catholic faith. His masterpiece, *Brideshead Revisited*, was followed by many works in which Catholic characters continue to illustrate the satisfying nature of Catholic practice, fidelity and even sanctity. Even though both writers may fall short as preachers of the faith, their work of imaginative writing has acted as a stimulus to spiritual reflection. In Ker's judgement, Waugh will better stand the test of time because of his greater consistency.

A similar discussion could be developed around the great fictional writers of 20th Century France. The novels of Francois Mauriac and Georges Bernanos, for example, showed the reality of Catholic Christian life to their readers as belonging to the orders of both nature and grace. Indeed, the signature work of Bernanos, *Diary of a Country Priest*, ends with the vital words, 'all is grace', which sum up the truth, goodness and beauty of a priest's life, and the life of any faithful Christian. The poetry and drama of Paul Claudel parallel this pervasive spirit in French literature, in particular in the two powerful plays, *Dialogue of the Carmelites* and *The Annunciation to Mary*, which placed Catholic theology, spirituality and even mysticism centre-stage in French literary life. As an interesting footnote, it has recently been commented that French culture has lost this voice of philosophical and spiritual profundity, something for which there is a nostalgia today, as evidenced by the public acclaim for the comparatively lightweight media philosopher Bernard - Henri Lévy (aka BHL!).

Film, drama and the spiritual imagination – It is the province of the film to be a work of imagination in the most literal sense. We see an image which is not the reality it reflects, or even the fantasy that it transmits. It is a human construction at two removes from any possible reality, and the space between the reality and the cinematic performance is all imagination. This work is of several strands, intellectual, moral, technical and so forth, all of them works of imagination. The intellectual includes the researching and development of the main guiding ideas and all the organisational elements of production. The moral includes the purposes of the film, what it is intended that it should bring to its audience and what response is hoped for from them. The technical includes everything that goes to make the film as an artifact, and is often itself a work of considerable imagination and innovation. And finally, the performance of the actors brings into play all the qualities of imaginative communication and the unique personalities of particular individuals.

It is the imagination that is the battleground for feelings, convictions and conversion of the heart. The work of imagination is in a sense sacramental, since it makes present, or enfleshes the good, beautiful and true by means of a kind of internal theology. What guides the imagination? In large part it is the values of the director and others inventing the film, including any particular sources. The intellectual, moral and technical qualities of the director are crucial, and it is these that are especially rewarded in prizes given to films or in the appreciations of the critics. The director is an artist. He or she is not bound by reality, but has a licence to provide images that convey ideas, impressions and insights. A film is not a documentary. There is no right way to render it. How it is constructed is subject to the creative genius of the director and the others involved, especially of course the actors, and the degree of harmony between them.

All these features apply even where the only intention of the director is to entertain, since entertainment is not independent of moral values. How does he or she entertain? What means are morally legitimate? We acknowledge canons in these matters since we have a degree of censorship even in secular societies, when, for example, censors restrict the viewing of a film by age or require cuts for a range of moral reasons. Similarly, people most frequently take a decision to see a film based upon what they have learnt of it beforehand, and this too is in part a moral decision. If the film treats matters of sexual morality lightly or in a degenerate or obscene fashion, or includes violence of an unusual degree, a person might decide not to see it. Or, in evaluating a film, a person might reflect upon what the film brought them that they value, whether aesthetically, intellectually or morally.

Any film with the elements of truth, goodness and beauty is capable of evangelising, or of transmitting and reinforcing the values to be found in gospel faith, whether this was intended by the director or not. For example, it has been pointed out by Terry Teachout, the American film critic, that many Westerns are highly moral in their story-line, and that they often pose the problem for a main character of whether or not they should take revenge for an injury they have suffered. The struggle over this issue is of course a moral one, and it is close to the Gospel, where we are taught not to seek vengeance and not to let the sun go down on our anger.

For all these reasons, the film is a work of art to be prized by the believer for its evangelising potential, whether this is explicit or only implicit. For example, although based on the works of a Catholic author, *The Lord of the Rings* is not an overtly religious film. It deals in mythic style with good and evil in such a way as to make good attractive and evil repulsive. The film-maker's imagination is used to explore the nature of truth, goodness and beauty in nature, in human personality and in events. The mission that Frodo undertakes can be taken as an allegory for the spiritual life. An essentially weak being continually returns to the task because its ultimate importance keeps being further revealed to him in moments of doubt or threatening despair. The beauty and goodness of the Shire are constantly recalled in contrast to the evil, violence and hatred of Mordor. The work is able thus to win over the conscience by its very beauty, which can be experienced as redemptive or as leading to moral conversion. It is a work of amazing imaginative power that stirs good feelings in the audience. It hints at ultimate values, and helps people to discover transcendence (TPAC, 11).

A remarkable example of an evangelising drama is provided by the Wintershall *The Life of Christ*, an amateur day-long production involving 250 actors which is presented for a week each year by a family living near London who were converted to the Catholic Church some years ago. A week's performances attracts 15000 visitors. These include large numbers of children and of non-believing adults. The event is very moving. Like the passion play of Oberammergau, it takes place in the open air, and the production moves around an estate with hillsides, lakes and constructed sets. This achieves a very imaginative and effective spiritual outreach. Its success, or better the blessing it received, can be estimated from the fact that one of the national television chains aired a five-part series on the making of the drama.

Radio, television and the Internet – Catholic radio stations like Radio Notre Dame in France demonstrate how religious broadcasting faithful to the Church can explore the Catholic faith positively and usefully. The televised media can be an ideal instrument for making the Gospel known. Education and various kinds of dialogue can be organised on a large scale. The example of the Eternal Word Television Network (EWTN) can be cited, with its teaching and exploration of Church doctrine and Scripture, presentation of the lives of saints, conversion stories, reports on current religious events or religious discussions, or spiritual phenomena such as Marian apparitions, and perhaps especially the transmission of regular or important liturgies. EWTN reaches virtually the whole planet through its satellite transmissions.

The Internet is of obvious concern to Christians because, while it is necessary for Christians to be well informed about the world and the Church, the living of the Gospel is more than a matter of knowing about things. In fact it is about knowing in a different way than having conscious information, and knowing how to respond, what to do, what is most worthwhile. For these reasons the Church has been very aware of the Internet and has made known its concerns in a series of documents, mainly from the Pontifical Council for Social Communications. However, official documents of the Church cannot give detailed directions as to the living out of the principles they identify. There is an immense work to be done by Christians in studying the world of social communications in specific settings, and finding out the implications for the use of such media for human welfare and spiritual development. The novelty and relevance of the Christian presence on the web as a means of contact between individuals and as a source of potentially life-changing information is, for example, evident in the penetration of the Internet in China and in the Islamic world.

The potential of these new media for sharing the Gospel creatively is enormous, but their technological development and exponential generation of data has so far outstripped the capacity to incorporate them into this work. Many Christian websites are quite primitive in this respect. They provide information, background reading and other resources, exhortations, prayers and devotional materials, but that is as far as many go. There are some that have introduced interactivity, through chat-rooms, email services, prayer intentions, as well as packaged advice and podcasts, and this is certainly the growing edge of the medium, but such approaches are demanding in the technical, imaginative and personal skills that they require, and these are still in short supply. This is therefore a priority area for investment of effort by the Church community.[13]

Secular websites hardly acknowledge religion except as a political category, or in the area of sensations and scandals. Yet an American study reported that 21% of web surfers have looked for religious or spiritual information on line, more, for example, than used internet banking. That is, more than two million surfers a day. One American vocations director said that 'the Internet is the way young people find information, so we have to be there and get the word out.' His website had received more than 12000 visits and 80 emails from men interested in the priesthood. We see from this that the web does not inevitably leave people mindless victims of pornography as so many accounts would suggest. There is a real danger of isolation and corruption, but there is also the potential for interactivity that can overcome these negative effects, and indeed offer unlimited opportunities for information and sharing the values of the Gospel. Pope John Paul appealed for such uses for the Internet:

I dare to summon the whole Church bravely to cross this new threshold, to put out into the deep of the Net, so that now as in the past the great engagement of the Gospel and culture may show to the world "the glory of God on the face of Christ."[14]

Beauty and the Church

The Church has consistently encouraged the beautiful, and Europe owes the Church an enormous debt for the great heritage of art, architecture, literature and the whole panoply of culture which was seen as both reflecting God's glory and contributing to it, whatever other human motives may have been at play at the same time. Some believe that this influence of the Church was an essentially conservative or classical one, keeping the arts in check, rejecting the new in favour of established forms, but it is not difficult to make the contrary argument through the great accomplishments of towering innovators in culture who were welcomed by the Church down the ages, from Michelangelo and Dante to Mozart, Rouault, Matisse, and Tolkien. Where would the list end? Each of us could give our own examples of media productions that 'evoke and glorify the transcendent mystery of God' (CCC, 2502) and allow a meeting of faith and culture in a new synthesis by bringing to light the goodness, truth and beauty of the Creator and his creation. In its own culture the Church can offer a model of the evangelised culture, for example in sacred art, sculpture, music and architecture, liturgy, spiritual writings, and above all the Scriptures that reflect God most closely in his transcendental attributes, and can potentially provide a meeting place for believers and unbelievers, where those who have a message they believe God wishes them to pass on can encounter those who feel an unsatisfied but genuine spiritual need.

Illustrations in a number of areas easily come to mind.

Liturgy and music – There is a risk even in the Church that art usurps the role of religion, precisely because it is taken as the beautiful, but separated from the true and the good. Thus, liturgy can abandon its vocation of being in the presence of the transcendent God, in order to feature the community, the evanescent, the popular, a kind of liturgy-lite. The persistence of creative art, aware of the past but able to continue to find new expression, is of key importance to the liturgy. As John Paul II points out, Gregorian chant, with its inspired modulations, became the music of the Church's faith in the liturgical celebration of the sacred mysteries. (LA, 7). Similarly, today the work of those who compose new music and hymns, or find new ways of using beautiful ways of praising God, is an essential contribution to liturgy. In his book *Ce Pape est un don de Dieu* Cardinal Poupard gives many examples of such work, but the most striking one is of Verdi's *Requiem,* which he arranged to be performed as part of the Eucharistic liturgy for the first time, to celebrate the centenary of Verdi's death.[15] He notes that the work is often performed in concert halls and churches, but never up to that time in a Requiem Mass. He reached agreement with maestro Gianluigi Gelmetti of the Rome Opera for a performance in the basilica of Santa Maria in Trastevere on the day of the anniversary, and continues:

> More than a hundred musicians, counting orchestra and choir, lifted us up in a unanimous prayer. The Word of God proclaimed in the Eucharist found a perfect accompaniment in Verdi's music. Paul's words to the Corinthians, 'In a moment, in the twinkling of an eye,... the

trumpet will sound and the dead will be raised imperishable' (1 Cor 15:52), were greeted with the overwhelming trumpeting of the 'Tuba mirum'. And the Day of the Last Judgement, described by Jesus in John's Gospel, chapter 5, was given a dramatic and gripping relief by the sound of the 'Rex tremendae majestatis', before Verdi's music calmed us gently in the vision of the divine mystery of the 'Lux aeterna'. My homily could only be a prayer: Listening to Verdi's Requiem, we are brought to contemplate your majesty, Lord, to admire your power and to rejoice in your love. This sublime music takes us into the last times inaugurated by Christ, alpha and omega, when the last trumpet will sound and we will all be transformed to become like you, when the dead will no longer hear the voices of men and their marvellous music, but instead the voice of the Son of God as they gaze on his radiant face. And those who see him will live for ever.

Cardinal Poupard concludes:

Through this Eucharistic celebration we overcame the pointless dispute about whether this music is more suited to theatre or church. We lived it as a prayer inspired by the singing of the soloists and the choir and by the music of the orchestral instruments, matchless interpreters, with Verdi himself, of the mystery of man and the mystery of God.

The liturgy, when carried out well, is perhaps the most effective way to involve truth, goodness and beauty in the process of uniting people to God. This is its purpose, after all. It uses prayer of different types, for example, praise and thanksgiving, it contains colour, music and choral harmonies.It has moments of solemnity, silence and festival. Liturgy can be compared in many ways to the media. It has settings, forms, rituals, texts, originators and receivers, and above all it has a conscious, clear and positive message, which is more than can often be said for the secular media. While it is one of the aspirations of the secular media to become more two-way, through audience participation, community-based programming, and so forth, it could be said that the liturgy has done all of this and takes it for granted.

However, there is no doubt that attention to the media suggests valuable ways to think about certain aspects of liturgy. When a media production is artistically beautiful and has technical coherence and moral integrity, its power is enormous, and people can feel a shift in their consciousness as the message offered sinks in. In a similar way, the language, the music, the directing of the ceremonies, the clarity of the sound system, the adequacy of the guidance given to the congregation, the inspirational quality of the prayers, the reverence of the atmosphere, and the depth of the reflection offered in homilies and other addresses, can all help make the impact of a liturgical function more complete and convincing. What is being said here is that we should recognise the communication dimension of the liturgy. It is a false piety to rely entirely upon the sacramental aspect, the purely spiritual significance of liturgy, just as it would be impious to turn the liturgy into mere theatre or concert. The reason why we need to reflect upon this aspect is that we can thereby enhance the everyday value of the liturgy as a means of instruction and spiritual development. The values represented by the liturgy are in fact the basic values of the Gospel and the faith, that is, the spiritual values of truth and awareness of the transcendent.

Beauty in the Word of God – There can be little doubt that the Old Testament in particular contains elements of world literature that count among the most beautiful writing in existence. It is writing that has inspired creators of beauty in so many areas: 'Sacred Scripture has thus become a sort of "immense vocabulary" (Paul Claudel) and "iconographic atlas" (Marc Chagall), from which both Christian culture and art have drawn.' (LA, 5). We can re-read so many biblical accounts for their pure truth, beauty and goodness as they speak of the lives of the patriarchs, from Abraham's sacrifice to the death of Moses, the transcendent nature of God and insights into the human soul in the psalms, the beauty of human love mirroring divine love in *The Song of Songs*, and the poetry and integrity of the songs of the suffering servant in *Isaiah*.

The beauty of the New Testament is different; it is hardly to be associated with poetry, descriptions of natural beauty, flights of imagination or other characteristic features of literature, however limpid, vivid, essential and beautiful its language, and yet it is filled with elements of the transcendentals, such as Paul expounding gospel truth and moral values and the *Book of Revelation* with its supreme vision of the beauty of the transcendent, and its picture of glory and justice in the parousia. However it is especially in the Gospels that the clearest features of the transcendentals can be discerned, as in the beauty of the birth narratives that have inspired the greatest works of art, the dense, multi-layered, yet sublimely simple parables, the eternal truths of the Sermon on the Mount, the revelations of the Trinity in the supper discourses, the divine goodness of the Eucharist and Calvary, and the mystical and symbolic, rather than rational statements of truth.

Beauty and nature - God the Creator has given us the world, which, from the simplest particle to the complexity and glory of the human being, expresses his love, his beauty and the truth about himself. All aspects of creation are important for us to approach God, and certainly not least that aspect which involves understanding, in however limited a form, something of the elegant workings and characteristics of the material universe. It has been cogently argued that science was best able to develop in the Christian world rather than elsewhere because of the Christian acceptance of a God of supreme reason and consistency rather than a God who was arbitrary in the use of his powers. Thus, the philosophers of science Stanley Jaki and Peter Hodgson have argued that science owes a debt to Christian faith. The Islamic understanding of God, on the other hand, is that he is arbitrary in his will and that creation inevitably mirrors this. Without faith in the rational order of creation science is impossible, because inconceivable.

The Catholic Church places reliance upon the notion of natural law, and the power of human reason to recognise the divine reality. The thomistic proofs of the existence of God were proofs by reason. The teaching of the Church councils and the work of scholars up to the present day retain this emphasis on the virtues of human reason. However, it is important to acknowledge that although the unaided mind can know God in his works, as the Catholic Church following St Paul teaches, it cannot approach God except where grace builds on nature, or inspiration makes use of human intelligence according to God's design to lead us to the truth. In seeking the expression of truth in culture we must include the work of scientific minds, whose intelligence, imaginativeness and perseverance have reflected and extended the Creator's work, or have made it more apparent to us. Science reveals God's power for the mind to see in the things he has made, especially as it indicates as God's action what secular science thought was the discovery of what was merely natural or, in the case of inventions, was even man's achievement. To help science to do this work of revealing God more intentionally is also to evangelise.

We can generalise this idea to the search through the works of the greater culture of science and the intellectual disciplines, politics and the whole life of the city. In all of these areas human intelligence, creativity and imagination seek meaning and purpose, and carry through positive and creative works, but this effort is prompted by God. Man is created as *capax Dei* (CCC, chap. 1), and God will always incite him to find his divine origin and destiny. Such work may be blinkered and fumbling, but the work of the evangeliser is once again to shed light, to indicate connections, to propose paths, interpretations, findings and conclusions, where secular efforts do not avail.[16]

We need to move to a stage in human research where science and Christian faith work collaboratively. This began to happen in the Middle Ages, but the link was broken by the Enlightenment. If we come back to a union of science and faith, and indeed of faith and reason more generally, it seems that we could expect a new age of understanding and development. A world with new forms of renewable energy, respect for life, care for the environment, and with an ethical foundation of philosophical and theological understanding, would be of far greater benefit to humanity than a science that is at the whim of utilitarian values or none at all. In the meantime, it is not for faith to withdraw shame-facedly from an encounter with science, but rather for it to show itself to be the source of questioning, of positive criticism, of encouragement to ethical debate, and of prophetic warning about the self-destructive tendencies of a science that lacks the wisdom of faith in a meaningful and purposeful universe.[17] The most promising aspect of this area is the integration of faith with science, but especially when we take it up from the perspective of faith to see where faith can contribute to science. Scientists may be tempted to regard science as self-sufficient, but this leads to an impoverished and finally unproductive or even dangerous science. It is not enough to speak of a natural theology, one that seeks to reconcile scientific and theological ideas. We need to go to the point at which human needs and values can be brought to bear on science, to check and guide it, to restrain and train its otherwise volatile momentum. This is the point about a holistic way of thinking, the complementarity of science and faith, or science and religion. This complementarity is a view that represents hope for the future. A science that is guided by faith can find so much more to celebrate, discover and develop.

But the human imagination ranges much wider. Science, while it can include important values such as integrity, or emotions such as awe, is strictly bound by its subject-matter. It can only report what it finds. In the arts, music and literature, and also in the activities of social life and relationships, and the raising of the heart and mind in prayer, while natural creation provides a starting-point, this limitation does not apply. The human imagination provides the most obvious evidence of our spiritual nature, and has no limits. It can explore infinitely. Indeed it can fly to God himself, and can uncover his attributes of truth, goodness and beauty in thought or through whatever medium it chooses.

A related human quality more familiar in the secular sphere than the religious is that of *creativity*, which is seen as an admirable characteristic of those who make original contributions to culture and science. Although we do not create from nothing, even as artists, thinkers, and writers making use of creative imagination, we do participate in God's creative work when we 'magnify', that is, reveal and extol, the glory of his creation. It is clear to the believer that human creativity is the reproduction of the Creator's work, our imitation of him in science, in the arts, and in our sensitivity to his beauty, truth and goodness. Indeed, it is in the act of creative work that the artist can apprehend something of the divine:

> *All artists experience the unbridgeable gap which lies between the work of their hands, however successful it may be, and the dazzling perfection of the beauty glimpsed in the ardour of the creative moment: what they manage to express in their painting, their sculpting, their creating is no more than a glimmer of the splendour which flared for a moment before the eyes of their spirit.* (LA, 6)

Nor is this activity of appreciation of God through creation or exploration of his truth, goodness and beauty through creativity and the imagination the special preserve of gifted individuals. It provides our ordinary way to approach God. It is sufficient to have an open mind, one that can perceive God in his creation humbly and gratefully. This quality in human beings is not universal, of course, because many are deliberately closed through pride, fear, or the corruption of their moral lives, or even through indifference. In such a state a person might engage in science or in the works of imagination to enhance their own importance or to satisfy a mere urge of curiosity or obsession with a particular material. Such a person needs the liberation of faith, the awareness that it is God who has created the reality confronting them, and that it is through God that they will come to know it and understand it, or represent it in some artistic form most fully and most perfectly within the limitations of the human mind.

It will be apparent that the argument of this chapter implies a call to action. While it is true that the appreciation of God and his works in prayer of adoration or thanksgiving is an appropriate way to give him glory, the believer is also called to be a co-creator with God by doing and making what will echo his truth, goodness and beauty. This activity must include engaging with the world of secular arts, as Pope John Paul II enjoins:

> *new artistic expressions of the faith should be promoted through a constant dialogue with those engaged in the arts... because artistic beauty, as a sort of echo of the Spirit of God, is a symbol pointing to the mystery, an*

invitation to seek out the face of God made visible in Jesus of Nazareth. (EE, 60)

A new culture is discernible here, one that is close in spirit, I believe, to what John Paul called for in *Novo Millennio Ineunte*. It is a culture of life, not just in the sense that it promotes values that are consistent with Church teaching on moral and ethical issues, but rather as a way of life with its own internal dynamism, spurred on by the faith of the Gospel into a deeper sense of the richness of its truth and its meaning for culture and human relationships. In thus coming to value reflection, imagination, beauty and holiness, not merely intellectually, but spiritually and practically, Christians can both play an active part in civil society and contribute to the work of the new evangelisation that includes the redeeming of contemporary culture.

NOTES

[1]Benedict XVI, Message to the Communion and Liberation Meeting, Rimini, 2002.

[2]Hans Urs von Balthasar, *The Glory of the Lord: a Theological Aesthetics*. Edinburgh: T. and T. Clark, 1985. See especially his study of Dante, John of the Cross, Pascal and Hopkins. The first three showed the human being struggling for understanding, light and grace before their gradual enlightenment, while Hopkins finds the Creator in all that he has made.

[3]John Saward, *The Beauty of Holiness and the Holiness of Beauty*. San Francisco: Ignatius Press, 1997.

[4]Scruton, op.cit, p.

[5]Chiara Lubich, 'Towards a theology and philosophy of unity', in David Schindler, ed., *An Introduction to the Abba School*. New York: New City Press, 2002, p 35

[6] Benedict XV, op. cit.

[7]Scruton, op. cit., p 29

[8]Saward, p. 36 et passim.

[9]Michael Mayne, *This Sunrise of Wonder: a Quest for God in Art and Nature*. London: Fount, 1995.

[10]Gabriele Finaldi, *'Seeing Salvation: the image of Christ'*, The Pastoral Review, April, 2005

[11]Pope Benedict XVI, op.cit.

[12]Ian Ker, *The Catholic Revival in English Literature:* 1845-1961. Leominster: Gracewing, 2003, pp. 1-2. A similar study has been published by Joseph Pearce, *Literary Giants; Literary Catholics*. San Francisco: Ignatius Press, 2005

[13]Some examples of Internet resources for evangelisation are listed at the end of the book, but the two websites set up by the Catholic Agency to Support Evangelisation (CASE) provide a model of the genre.

[14]John Paul II, Message for 36th World Communications Day

[15]Cardinal Paul Poupard, *Ce Pape est un don de Dieu*. Paris: Plon/Mame, 2001.

[16]see Andrew Greeley, The Catholic Imagination (Berkeley: Univ of California Press, 2000 and also James Harvey and Anthony Carroll, *On the Way to Life*. London: Catholic Education Service, 2005. The latter emphasise the sacramental (or incarnational) dimension of the Catholic imagination.

[17]Wiker, B. and Witt, J. *A Meaningful World: How the Arts and Sciences Reveal the Genius of Nature*. Westmont, Ill., InterVarisity Press, 2006.

CHAPTER TEN

Renewing the Face of the Earth

THE POINT HAS been continually and deliberately made that the work of evangelising culture is of the Holy Spirit, and therefore it is the spiritual aspect of the activity that is crucial. Indeed, God has already kept his promises, and if our faith and trust are sufficient we will see them carried to fruition. The spiritual dimension, though primary, is being discussed in conclusion, for its importance will more easily emerge in the synthesis of human effort and divine inspiration. There is no telling of the truth, no recognition or expression of beauty, no living of goodness without the grace and inspiration of the Holy Spirit, but in fact he has already provided for all this; that has been his mission from the beginning.

There are several aspects to the task by which humanity accomplishes its part in the divine plan for bringing the Gospel to the world, but in their essence they are captured by St Paul's appeal to the Athenians to repent and live righteously.

Step seven
renewing the face of the earth
in the power of the Holy Spirit

If the insights and truths of the Gospel are to be proposed to the secular culture, it is necessary to discern how the good seeds can best be implanted, and the resources available must be identified and deployed, thus making room for all the gifts of the Spirit. Secondly, any spiritual service to the community involves developing and nurturing new relationships, inspiring a shared vision through work of reconciliation, and broadening the community to build a civilisation of love, in which the life of Christ can be realised and spread. Thirdly, the existence of such focal points of communion can only be the beginning of a process of dissemination through prayerful intercession for the secular world and for unbelievers. And lastly, the contemplation of God, the seeking of his face, and the welcoming of his Spirit in a new Pentecost of truth and love, are already ushering in the reign of God, helping to build it on earth as the first stage of the promised eternal life of paradise.

The new Pentecost

There is a human tendency, under the influence of sinfulness, to misunderstand and corrupt God's gifts, and this is the picture we see in much of the world today. The fresh impetus needed to understand, correct and elaborate a new vision of reality corresponding to God's will and revelation is only possible by grace. While sharing the Gospel is an obligation for all Christians, it is not something that they can undertake in their own strength. The 'principal agent' of this work is the Holy Spirit: 'it is he who in the depths of consciences causes the word of salvation to be accepted and understood.' (EN, 75). The entire work of the spreading and developing of faith in God and his redemptive plan for humanity is energised and guided by the Holy Spirit, from the mission *ad gentes* and the new evangelisation to the reconciliation, catechesis and formation of new Christians. So it is important for Christians to realise that, in effect, the Holy Spirit has already evangelised the culture through the doctrines of the faith, the thoughts, aesthetic character and the moral sense of the prayers of the Church, the liturgy, and above all through the Bible. These are replete with worked out examples of cultures being evangelised. They need only to be brought to light.

There is a lack of a pastoral theology of the Holy Spirit common to seminary education, catechesis and parochial life, such that the Church continues to be spiritually handicapped, even while Pope John Paul continually appealed for an openness to the Spirit as the way to holiness and to the renewal of the Church. The cost of inadequate catechesis on the Holy Spirit in the Church is considerable. It affects the spiritual renewal of Catholic Christians, it restrains ecumenism, it hobbles evangelisation, it contributes to the persistent lack of a sense of sin and desire for repentance and consequent neglect of the sacrament of reconciliation; it undermines faith in spiritual and physical healing, belief in deliverance and in the pervasive reality of spiritual warfare; and it breeds excessive caution and even scepticism concerning prophetic and other charismatic gifts and mystical events that none the less seem so powerful in nourishing the faith and spiritual vitality of believers. What this amounts to is a definite repudiation of the notion of an inward-looking Christian community. In thought, word, action and prayer the Christian is called to evangelise, that is, to be ready to give an account of his faith, in season and out of season. This is so important to emphasise because of the evident fact that many Christians are discouraged, fearful of hostility or ridicule, or simply feel inadequate to the task. It is true that these dangers and weaknesses are not illusions. They exist. But the nature of faith is not to work from human possibilities or impossibilities but from divine omnipotence. It is only necessary to look at certain current initiatives in the Catholic world to see clearly that God favours the brave.

Many of the new ecclesial movements are known for their strong orthodoxy and emphasis upon the Eucharist, Marian devotion and loyalty to the Holy See. Pope John Paul called attention specifically to the way in which these groups 'give the Church a vitality that is God's gift'. He recalled that, while Church harmony is to be respected, the Church must always heed St Paul's warning: 'Do not quench the Spirit'. (1Thess 5:19) He added:

This is a fundamental principle not only for the endless theological investigation of Christian truth, but also for Christian dialogue with other philosophies, cultures and religions. (NMI, 56)

The new movements need the support and collaboration of the members of Church parishes if they are not to be discouraged, but some unfortunate incidents have raised uncomfortable questions about local churches and their leaders. What is such leaders' image of the new ecclesial communities and associations such as Youth 2000 or the Neo-catechumenal Way? Are they not convinced by the evidence that the Holy Spirit has moved the young to contribute to the future of the Church? If young people's desires for the Church are negated, this condemns to frustration all their efforts at inspiring a renewal of faith, because it suggests that they are not taken seriously enough to inspire genuine hope.

The new evangelisation expresses the desire for a new Pentecost uttered by Pope John XXIII when he announced the calling of the Second Vatican Council. It is an act of faith in the Holy Spirit who inspires not only the audacity of this very prayer, but the sometimes uncomfortable newness of the new evangelisation in *ardour, method* and *expression*. This work is however centred upon Scripture and the teaching of the Church. It represents the promise of a new Covenant, comparable to but surpassing the Messianic promise of the old Covenant. It has a character that is Trinitarian, because community centred, Christocentric because concerned with the preaching of Christ's Gospel, and Marian, because Mary is the original model of the one who enables the earthly epiphany of God.

Mary, Spouse of the Holy Spirit – The Marian dimension, the love, the maternal tenderness, that absorb without any discord the tensions between theories, offices and methods of government in the Church, that defuse controversy and conflict in a humble submission and peacefulness, leave us united more by our belonging to Jesus than divided by our human affiliations and experiences. Mary is full of grace, she symbolises the mystical Church without spot or wrinkle, that is ever on our horizon as a guide. This Star of the new Evangelisation provides a sure guide and compass-bearing, as one who is not disturbed by the storms of sin. She calls us to faith, hope and love. She is the mirror of the Church,

Cantalamessa says, and also the way by which the Holy Spirit leads us to Jesus. Mary prayed in the Upper Room. Would the spiritual mother of mankind not have prayed in the Spirit for exactly those blessings that Jesus sought when he addressed the Father at the Last Supper, the blessings that we so long for today: eternal life for believers in his name, the fruits of their mission to the world, and the unity of all in the truth, goodness and beauty of the Blessed Trinity?

Could there be a better time to announce the good news, to believe that the Church can revive, be renewed spiritually, be restored to purity, be unified as one Christian body in the world, as one mystical body of Christ? This is the message of Mary, brought to the world today especially through the enormous flow of pilgrims to Guadalupe, Fatima, Medjugorje and other shrines. But it is not a message the Blessed Mother invents. It is one of which she reminds us, because in proclaiming God's love and mercy, in assuring us of his grace and pardon, Mary remains the Mother of the Incarnate God, Jesus Christ, the submissive daughter of the Father, and the inspired Spouse of the regenerating Spirit of God. She is the one who is full of grace and, as Pope John Paul recalled in several passages in TMA, entirely open to the Holy Spirit, always living in the presence of God, filled with his inspiration, a model of faith, hope and love leading people to her Son through prayer, fasting and peace.

Preparing for a new Pentecost - A new Pentecost is both a hope of the evangelist and an evident reality in our world. A Pentecostal perspective is fully discernible in teaching of the Magisterium, especially in the documents of Vatican II and the writings of Pope John Paul II, in insightful recent works by different Christian writers such as Peter Hocken, including Catholic charismatic sources, and in reports of Christian experience in the ministries of healing and deliverance.[1] Such writers perceive benefits for the Church that could come from an expansion of vision to take fuller account of the work of the Holy Spirit in what God plans for the human world. Pope John Paul specifically acknowledged this theological need when he called for:

...a renewed appreciation of the presence and activity of the Spirit, who acts within the Church both in the sacraments, especially in confirmation, and in the variety of charisms, roles and ministries which he inspires for the good of the Church... (TMA, 45)

He also constantly spoke of the new communities as a hope for the Church, seeing them as a work of the Spirit, and 'a new Pentecost', both bringing their members to Christ and bringing Christ to others in the world through their efforts to witness to the Gospel.

Thanks to the charismatic movement, many Christians, men and women, youths and adults, have rediscovered Pentecost as a living and present reality in their daily life.... I desire that the spirituality of Pentecost be spread in the Church, as a renewed thrust of prayer, holiness, communion and proclamation.[2]

The capillary action to which the Church is subject through these 'Pentecostal' or charismatic influences ensures the dissemination of their evangelising action. The renewal of scriptural prayer and community spirituality, of liturgy, of lifestyle, of sacred art, of Eucharistic and Marian devotion, of shrines and pilgrimages, do not mean a going back to the past in a conservative movement, but a re-presenting of Christ and his call to conversion to the world:

By putting Christ back as the keystone of existence and restoring the place of reason enlightened by faith, a pastoral approach to culture could strengthen Christian identity by a clear and enthusiastic invitation to holiness. (TPAC, 23)

The evangeliser is led to humility and trust in God. For if we have in mind the general apostasy that afflicts most of the older Christian countries, it is nothing less than 'Pentecostal' grace that can find and restore all the dysfunctional trails that have led people away from God.

A spirituality of communion – If pastors want a renewed Church, they need to preach it, recognising the complementarity of the sacramental and Pentecostal orders of grace. They must call upon the people to open their hearts to the Holy Spirit, to accept the Lordship of Christ in every area of their lives, and to allow God to have his way, believing that his plans for the world are better than those we ourselves could ever imagine.[3] This would be to enter into a Trinitarian communion of life, one that recognises the truth and love that unite the Godhead and constitute our essential mission and destiny as Christians and as Church. Pope John Paul II identified this unifying communion by contrasting the two dimensions of the Church which were outlined in Chapter 8, which he calls hierarchical and spiritual:

> *While the wisdom of the law, by providing precise rules for participation, attests to the hierarchical structure of the Church and averts any temptation to arbitrariness or unjustified claims, the spirituality of communion, by prompting a trust and openness wholly in accord with the dignity and responsibility of every member of the People of God, supplies institutional reality with a soul.*
> (NMI, 45)

The spiritual dimension must be seen as primary, he continues, otherwise 'external structures of communion will serve very little purpose' (NMI, 43). The Pope challenged the Church to acknowledge not just its conventional hierarchical features but also the great diversity of gifts whose common purpose is to bind the Church into one body:

> *Such a vision of communion is closely linked to the Christian community's ability to make room for all the gifts of the Spirit. The unity of the Church is not uniformity, but an organic blending of legitimate diversities. It is the reality of many members joined in a single body, the one Body of Christ. (NMI, 46)*

But beyond the spiritual challenge to each believer, NMI indicates that there are a number of pastoral priorities that must be met by the Church collectively and globally. The Apostolic Letter's paragraph on the spirituality of communion may be the most prophetic in the whole document for its implications in relation to the wider human family, the gathering into unity of all the children of God. There are four main elements. First, the mystical one involves recognising the Trinitarian source of our human family:

> *...the heart's contemplation of the mystery of the Trinity dwelling in us, and whose light we must also be able to see shining on the face of the brothers and sisters around us.* (NMI, 43)

The spirituality of communion derives from the Trinity. The Trinity is a spirituality of communion, *the* spirituality of communion. In having the disposition to reach out in love, service, giving, receiving, exchanging, to value, to empower or to endorse, we live out the Trinitarian life. Thus, this spirituality is about living the present moment of seeing, understanding and loving in God.

Then, there are three practical ways of doing God's work by thinking, seeing and doing what the Gospel demands of us: thinking of our brothers and sisters in faith within the profound unity of the Mystical Body, and therefore as 'those who are a part of me'; seeing what is positive in others, to welcome it and prize it as a gift from God; and 'to make room for our brothers and sisters...' and 'resisting the selfish temptations which constantly beset us and provoke competition, careerism, distrust and jealousy.' (NMI, 43) Entering into a spirituality of communion is seeking holiness at the level of the whole community of faith, the Church, and indeed globally. Of its nature Christianity is cosmic in scale. It acknowledges a God who is universal and almighty. Therefore anything less than a global and holistic approach to spiritual and philosophical, let alone political questions, is unacceptable. The Christian will always want to go further to see the greater context, to see even beyond life on earth, which only the religions do, and where faith alone can offer explanations and counsel. It refers to all that we do to build peace, to ensure unity of minds and hearts, and to be models of loyalty to the wider Church and the world in love and service. It offers a possibility of renewal to the whole Church, at a time when many Christians are welcoming the Holy Spirit in a new way.

An evangelised culture – A 'spirituality of communion' is so much more than a culture; it is an evangelised culture. Christian culture connects to the Absolute, which moors it, and has a purpose or destination, in seeing itself essentially as a journey by people who are seeking eternal salvation. One of the characteristics of this culture is that its adherents are not merely individuals since theologically they are part of the Body of Christ. They cannot come alone to salvation, but only as part of the Church, the ark of salvation. The coherence of Christian culture, therefore, is a belonging together in Christ. And the acknowledgement of this belongingness is a spirituality of Christian communion. This is different from any secular culture, since its source is supernatural. It depends upon the virtue of love received from God, and given to God and to each other because of everyone's origin in God. But it is still a culture; it is growing; it gives meaning and purpose to common life. A spirituality of communion gives people a motive not only for staying together in mutual service, but for action, for development, and for seeking God as fulfilment. This is why Pope John Paul appealed to it as the way that the people of

God choose, act, and define themselves, whether as local communities, as Church or as a global family.

The living out of this spirituality in daily life can lead to renewal in society, through the family and Christian relationships, through the contributions of caring and of intellectual and creative work, and the exercising of civic responsibilities. The work of evangelising culture is effected in all these contexts, because the most important values in human life concern how we live with each other and how we relate personally, socially and spiritually. Involved in this is our sense of our own identity, the value we attach to the human being, our view of the value and purposes of human life and social relations, our responsibility for each other in the wider community as well as in terms of the higher values of sacrifice, self-donation and fidelity to a religious creed. The Christian injunction to love our neighbour is simply the practical implication of these values. Flowing from the basic principle of respect and love for each human being, and for life itself as the gift of the Creator, are many implications that affect how we see each other and behave towards each other.

The new conditions that Christians face in the world have a global dimension that challenges administrative and cultural boundaries and calls them to have a corresponding global vision and concern:

Today we must courageously face a situation which is becoming increasingly diversified and demanding, in the context of "globalization" and of the consequent new and uncertain mingling of peoples and cultures. (NMI, 40)

According to the Pope there are a number of related ethical considerations: globalisation must not be a new form of colonialism; it must not imply the relativisation of all values; and it must not mean the dismissal of the individual value of the human person.

Our world is entering the new millennium burdened by the contradictions of an economic, cultural and technological progress which offers immense possibilities to a fortunate few, while leaving millions of others not only on the margins of progress but in living conditions far below the minimum demanded by human dignity. How can it be that even today there are still people dying of hunger? Condemned to illiteracy? Lacking the most basic medical care? Without a roof over their heads? (NMI, 50)

Another feature of globalisation is the spread of secular and religious ideologies that oppose Christianity. The Vatican speaks of Christianophobia, the rejection of Christian faith and values, the persecution of Christians in many parts of the world, and the writing out from history of Christian civilisation.

Therefore among the global priorities that Pope John Paul identified were the religious ones of ecumenism and interreligious dialogue. Christians must never abandon their hopes, prayers and initiatives for the full unity of the Church, and a concern for ecumenism must feature in every Christian's life. However, the relationships between those of different world religions, a pastoral area in which relatively few can claim to have been really active, also need to be accorded greater importance and linked to the dialogue with secular society and with non-believers. In this work Pope John Paul counselled 'openness, combined with careful discernment' (NMI, 56). That is, Christians need to avoid naivety, by becoming knowledgeable about other faiths and never compromising their own faith position by rushing to adopt common ground indiscriminately. The initiative of the European Congresses for the New Evangelisation provides an inspiring model. The succession of four separate annual congresses in Vienna, Paris, Lisbon and Budapest, has opened up a new vista in evangelisation. For example, the French congress, *Paris Toussaint* in November 2004, comprised 450 events, and brought Christian culture and the sharing of the Gospel to venues all over the city.

Furthermore, at the global level, we should 'stake everything on charity' (NMI, 49), in such areas as third world debt, ecology, peace and human rights, and pro-life values. Many in the Church, through their apostolic or secular activities, are in the front line of ethical discussion in evangelising or in social and political encounters. Have we focused sufficiently on our responsibility to speak with a powerful Christian voice on ethical issues, population questions, ecological and resource matters, and on religious rights and freedoms? This is a shared duty of all Catholics, requiring a new energy and approach, and finding effective ways to live and share the Gospel. While the word global might be taken by some as pointing to a dimension transcending personal responsibility, Christians know that their faith does not let them off so lightly. In the spiritual realm we all have global, indeed cosmic concerns. For instance, Christians pray for world peace without being political leaders and prayer for peace is certainly more availing than the unpeaceful wranglings of political leaders who claim to be seeking peace. Two remarkable examples of the effectiveness of spiritual witness to peace are found in the life of Pope John Paul, in his hosting of a meeting to pray for peace in Assisi with the leaders of many world religious leaders and, even more strikingly, in his role in the peaceful implosion of the Soviet Communist empire.

A final point takes us closer to the heart of Catholic Eucharistic faith. It is the path to holiness through communion with Jesus, and through him with the Blessed Trinity, that offers us entry into its own 'spirituality of communion', bringing the dimension of love into our lives and inspiring us constantly to share our faith with others. How do we play our part? The essence of it must be personal witness. Our own experience is the most convincing thing we have to offer. This does not downgrade Church doctrine, of course, but doctrine has to be assimilated by a willing heart and mind. What we are doing through our evangelising efforts is fostering this willingness. We can explain, but it is more important to inspire and, as Pope Paul said, we inspire more through the witness of our example than by simply teaching. This is why the evangelist has not simply to be a competent and knowledgeable teacher, but a believer in Christ who experiences a living relationship with him, and is able to share that experience with others in a movement that may begin as one-to-one, but then has to extend throughout the world.

The spirituality of communion is linked to the evangelising of culture because to evangelise culture is to revivify everything in the light of the Gospel. According to Chiara Lubich, founder of Focolare,

The point is that we need to bring God back to life in us, then keep him alive, and therefore overflow him on to others like bursts of life that revive the dead. And we need to keep him alive among us by loving one another... Then everything changes, politics, and art, education and religion, private life and recreation, everything.[4]

This communion links us through God's love to the company of saints as well as to our contemporaries. We are invited into the Trinity as the result of Christ's sacrificial love and his Eucharist restoring unity to the broken cosmos. This brokenness is evident in the incompleteness of our present world, the closed-off quality of human individualism, peacelessness and death. By sharing that condition through his Incarnation and his Passion, as Chiara Lubich points out, 'Jesus Forsaken' re-establishes unity with the whole of creation, beginning with humanity. This restoring and repairing process is shared by the Church and its members, so that, loving God, neighbour and creation, we are able to be part of the work of redemption.

We could not have a spirituality of communion that was itself inward-looking or elitist. Such a spirituality must take on all the evangelising dimensions of the divine work of salvation. No one and nothing is excluded from the Creator's love. However, this love does not compel; it only invites. Therefore human freedom allows us to resist the love and obedience to which we are called. But, at the same time, love does exert an influence over indifference, ignorance and hatred. This is the way of the Cross and it is also the way of gospel love, justice and peace. We cannot know the conclusion, but we are invited to walk the way and to help renew the face of the earth, inspired and guided by the Holy Spirit.

NOTES

[1]See Peter Hocken, *Blazing the Trail*. Stoke on Trent: Alive Publishing, 2001

[2]John Paul II in an address to pilgrims including Italian charismatic renewal, on 30 May 2004 (www.zenit.org)

[3]Raniero Cantalamessa, *Life in the Lordship of Christ*. London: Darton, Longman and Todd, 1992.

[4]Chiara Lubich, *'The Resurrection of Rome'*, in Schindler, op.cit., p101

CHAPTER ELEVEN

A Work of the Holy Spirit

How is secular society to be saved? Like the first disciples gathering in prayer with Mary the mother of Jesus, today's Christians are called to accept the leading of the Holy Spirit so as to be able to carry out Christ's commission to bring the Good News of salvation to the world.

The Spirit is the principal agent of the new evangelization. Hence it will be important to gain a renewed appreciation of the Spirit as the one who builds the kingdom of God within the course of history and prepares its full manifestation in Jesus Christ, stirring people's hearts and quickening in our world the seeds of the full salvation which will come at the end of time. (TMA, 45)

With so many restraints on faith, it is urgent that Catholic pastors be fully awake to the spiritual moment that we are living. Should they not be following Pope John Paul and preaching the new Springtime? Should they not be calling on the Lord for a Holy Spirit-empowered spirituality (of course there is no other kind), one that really anticipates a new, or a continuing Pentecost in the Church? Is the alternative not the unthinkable one that pastors have concluded that the promises of Christ before his ascension (Mark 16 and Luke 24) have been prorogued: that he will not send his Spirit; that believers will not be accompanied by signs; that there will not be healing; that the Gospel will not be preached to all nations?

We are led to the acknowledgement of a spiritual reality that is not some mere shadow of our human existence but is actually the primary reality. It is the reality that will continue when our earthly existence is over, either for us individually or as a race. The most fundamental understanding of the meaning and purpose of our lives is the gospel teaching that they serve to build God's Kingdom, that is, they are concerned above all with a work of preparation or transformation whereby our existence is purified, and, passing through the experience of sin, evil, sickness and death, by keeping focused upon God and his teachings in Christ, they return in holiness to their source. We do not see clearly how this occurs, but the Gospel shows us the way.

Following the Gospel, that is, the way, the truth and the life that Christ personified on earth, through the action of the Holy Spirit by which God's grace is made active in us, we come to hope and work for a reconciliation with our fellows and with God. This is the reality that constitutes his reign or Kingdom. Speaking to the Pontifical Council for Culture, Pope John Paul referred to the Kingdom dimension of renewal that gospel faith could bring to culture:

> *Faith in Christ gives cultures a new dimension, that of hope in God's Kingdom. It is the vocation of Christians to instil in the heart of cultures this hope for a new earth and a new heaven. For when hope fades, cultures die. Far from threatening or impoverishing cultures, the Gospel increases their joy and beauty, freedom and meaning, truth and goodness.*[1]

We see the beginnings of this transformation in human holiness, and we easily find examples of this both in great figures of our time and in our daily encounters. Hol iness leads to union with others as brothers and sisters in Christ, but also as adopted and redeemed sons and daughter of the Father. It is, as has been several times recalled, through the presence and activity of the Holy Spirit that the building of the Kingdom takes place, both the eternal Kingdom of God and his Reign on earth. This latter Kingdom is achieved by small steps, a seed in the ground, or some yeast. It is also something that is promised to the faithful, to the childlike, the poor, the peaceful, not to the denizens of earthly power (Matthew 5). This shows that it is truly God's work, in spite of humanity's efforts and pretensions. All that we can say is that our support for the Kingdom through prayer, faithfulness, playing our part in a humble way, relying upon God but using the gifts he has given us, are both part of this Kingdom and a means to bringing it about.

And what if this so greatly desired renewal begins to happen in such a way as to alter human priorities globally? What if people of 'every tribe and language and people and nation' (Rev 5:9), those that Jesus has redeemed, declared openly their spiritual needs? The Catholic Church would inevitably have an immense responsibility as the repository of the true faith. It could not fail, since it would be the best hope of all people that they should come under the Church's influence and guidance. But how could it be ensured that people would know the Church, be able to recognise it, approach it, and benefit from it? As things stand at the moment, the Church is largely unprepared, less approachable than it might be, often seeming to lack confidence in its teachings, and unused to making its voice heard in the marketplace. This is not of the nature of the Church, of course, because in times past and in some parts of the world today the Church has provided a haven for the perplexed and suffering. In most of the developed world, however, the Church today has effectively accepted its marginal standing in relation to the political and academic worlds and the media.

What would happen if people who have hitherto been too

proud to interest themselves in a God suddenly want to find out as quickly as possible about the Christian faith? They would need to be advised about where to go, what to read, to whom to speak. These and other enquirers would want to find someone in whom they can have confidence, who is not only informed but also formed, that is, spiritually minded, prayerful, and credible. Even more certainly, people would need to be led in prayer. They would know even less about prayer than they know about Christianity in the doctrinal sense, but their need for prayer would be more urgent. They would also need to have the Bible presented to them as a resource they can turn to directly.

I hope that this book has given a partial answer to such questions. Put another way, what has been said is directly concerned with how believing Christians could become more prepared to lead and to teach. The implications of this would need further working out, but clearly Christian people would have to be very active, possibly working full-time in churches providing programmes of explanation and formation, especially focussing on the Creed, the sacraments and spirituality. The work of evangelisation constituted by the seven steps, or some similar strategy, would also be the best form of preparation for any possible future scenario, and it would be a positive development for any practising Catholic to prepare for this kind of mission. It would mean becoming more familiar with resources and modes of explanation, and more confident in speaking directly about

Catholic belief, moral teaching and spiritual life. It must be the case that now is the time for Christians to commit themselves more wholeheartedly and prayerfully to this work, because the need is already discernible. Indeed, during the period of Pope John Paul's death and funeral it became quite palpable.

What would be the consequence if the work of evangelising culture is neglected? If Christians do not pay attention to this dimension of evangelisation it means that the very factors in the world that separate many people from God, cause them to fall away or discourage them from sharing their faith with others are left in place with their power to block the Gospel. The pressures that induce scepticism remain, and new generations will more easily be 'evangelised' by secular society and culture. Those who have declared that there is no such thing as society are ignoring how even the family is a social unit, as is the school, the Church or any of the myriad organisations that influence people's lives. While the individual is the locus of conversion, each person is subject to a variety of influences, pressures and constraints, and the work of evangelising culture acts upon these social and cultural influences, to encourage, inhibit or disarm them.

It is clear that the evangelising of culture is an essential part of this work since it is evangelising in the wider social, political and intellectual context. But it must have God's blessing; it must be within his will; and it must be fully expressive of his love. There is no evangelised culture, indeed no work of lasting value, that depends entirely upon autonomous human intentions and actions. Conversely, although there are gifts that attract attention because they seem so rich and fruitful, we are not the best judges of their value. The humblest efforts may be equally valuable and perhaps even more fruitful, because they are freer from vestiges of self-regard and ambition. This needs to be remembered even while we are impressed by what seem to be unique human achievements in the expression of goodness, truth and beauty.

The seven steps revisited

While the seven-step strategy for bringing the Gospel to life in culture must be seen as a simplified model, it does have the usefulness of helping us to understand a more complex process. One feature of the model may have surprised some readers. Its seven steps form what could be seen as a sociological beginning to a spiritual task, looking critically at culture and gradually bringing faith in the presence and activity of the Holy Spirit into the equation. Why prayer at the conclusion? Any Christian will know that prayer must be at the beginning, and therefore that the seven steps need to be seen as a circle, in which the appeal to the Holy Spirit which has been reached at the end is also at the start. Seeing the process this way opens our horizons, by allowing us to retrace the seven steps under the inspiration of the Holy

Spirit. The nature of the book has been to explore and enflesh an understanding of the evangelising of culture, not only seeing how this theme has been discussed in recent Church teaching but also, and perhaps more ambitiously, seeking to indicate how it can be supported and pursued by any committed Christian. Ho pefully, this has suggested in a plausible way some of the potential for bringing the Gospel into the lives and cultures of those who are working in their homes, local communities and parishes as well as through the intellectual and aesthetic channels of literary, artistic or political activity.

I embarked on this work out of a sense that a very important mission was awaiting Christians but that it had not been made sufficiently explicit for people to see how closely it related to how they were very often already living their lives. So, did it matter to write a book if the task was under way? The reader must judge from what has been said, but the view I have taken is that the distinction between bringing the Gospel to individuals and bringing the Gospel to cultures is an important one to identify, since this potentially larger vision can generate insights and release energy, and above all inspire hope for whole new dimensions of the Kingdom. I have sought to illustrate this by particular reference to the world of the young, of science, the media and the arts, but have also continually maintained that the approach did not preclude any committed Christian from valid and valuable participation as part of their ordinary apostolate in the world.

I end the book in a spirit of appreciation for the extraordinary range of teaching, building on embryonic insights in the documents of Vatican II, that Pope Paul VI and Pope John Paul II have left to illuminate the Church's reflection on culture and evangelisation. More than anyone else in our time, I am convinced that it has been Pope John Paul who has provided the vision that others are now called to adopt, namely that the message of the Gospel for today is not only that the Church exists to evangelise but that each of us is responsible for living as a witness to the Lord. I began with his exhortation to 'put out into the deep!' I hope that this work has gone some way towards exploring what this phrase first spoken by Jesus could mean in practice. Above all, I see it as referring to the unknown seas of a strange new culture in our world that is trying to live without God. This human enterprise is not of God's will. Instead, he invites everyone into his Kingdom, but they have to come of their own volition.

Christians are those who live in the world but who are not of the world, since they are already on their way to the Kingdom. However, t hey have received from Jesus the command to teach all nations, and so they cannot complete their journey without playing their part in bringing the good news of salvation to others. If others are living without God, then it is for Christians to draw them out of the darkness into the light. This is no mission impossible, or Jesus would not have died uttering the words: 'It is accomplished!' And this should not lead us to mere optimism that the task can be done, but rather to the certain hope that it is essentially already achieved, and awaits only our humble finishing touches!

NOTES

[1]John Paul II, Address to the Pontifical Council for Culture, 14 Mar 1997 (www.vatican.va)

ABBREVIATIONS

Church Document Abbreviations

AG *Ad Gentes*, in Flannery, A. ed., Vatican Council II. Leominster: Fowler Wright, 1975.

CCC *Catechism of the Catholic Church*

GDC *General Directory of Catechesis*

EN Pope Paul VI, *Evangelii Nuntiandi*. Catholic Truth Society, 1975.

EE Pope John Paul 11, *Ecclesia in Europa* (www.vatican.va,2003)

EV Pope John Paul II, *Evangelium Vitae* (Catholic Truth Society, 1995)

FR Pope John Paul II, *Fides et Ratio* (Catholic Truth Society, 1998)

LA Pope John Paul 11, *Letter to Artists* (www.vatican.va, 1999)

LG *Lumen Gentium,* in Flannery, op.cit.

NMI Pope John Paul II, *Novo Millennio Ineunte* (Catholic Truth Society, 2001)

RD Pope John Paul II, *The Rapid Development* (www.vatican.va, 2005)

RM Pope John Paul II *Redemptoris Missio* (Catholic Truth Society, 1991)

TMA Pope John Paul II, *Tertio Millennio Adveniente* (Catholic Truth Society, 1995)

TPAC Pontifical Council for Culture, *Towards a Pastoral Approach to Culture*. PCC, 1999.

VS Pope John Paul II, *Veritatis Splendor* (Catholic Truth Society, 1993)

SELECT BIBLIOGRAPHY AND INTERNET SOURCES

The listings below contain details of Church documents cited in the book, as well as those books which were most central to the work, and the websites found to be of most practical use. Some other works referred to for less essential reasons are detailed in chapter endnotes.

Church Documents

Catechism of the Catholic Church (London: Chapman, 1994)

Flannery A., ed., *Vatican Council II*. Leominster: Fowler Wright, 1975, including: *Lumen Gentium; Gaudium et Spes; Ad Gentes; Nostra Aetate*.

John Paul II   *Redemptoris Missio*. Catholic Truth Society, 1991.

                    Veritatis Splendor. Catholic Truth Society, 1993.

                    Crossing the Threshold of Hope. London: Jonathan Cape, 1994.

                    Evangelium Vitae. Catholic Truth Society,

1995.

Tertio Millennio Adveniente. Catholic Truth Society, 1995.

Fides et Ratio. Catholic Truth Society, 1998.

Letter to Artists. www.vatican.va, 1999.

Ecclesia in America. www.vatican.va, 1999.

Novo Millennio Ineunte. Catholic Truth Society, 2001.

Message for World Peace Day. www.vatican.va, 2002.

Ecclesia in Europa. www.vatican.va, 2003.

The Rapid Development. www.vatican.va, 2005.

Paul VI   *Evangelii Nuntiandi*. London: Catholic Truth Society, 1975.

Pontifical Council for Culture,

Towards a Pastoral Approach to Culture. Vatican: PCC, 1999.

Jesus Christ, the Bearer of the Water of Life: A Christian reflection on the 'New Age'. Vatican: PCC, 2003.

Pontifical Council for Justice and Peace, *Compendium of the Social Doctrine of the Church*. Vatican:PCJP, 2004.

Pontifical Council for Social Communications

Ethics in Advertising. Vatican: PCSC,1997.

Vatican: PCSC, 2000.

Ethics in Internet. Vatican: PCSC, 2002.

The Church and Internet. Vatican: PCSC, 2002.

General

Benedict XVI, *Values in a Time of Upheaval.* San Francisco: Ignatius Press, 2006.

Brechon, P. and Willaime, J-P., eds. *Médias et Religions en Miroir.* Paris: Presses Universitaires de France, 2000

Burrows, L. *The Fight for the Family.* Family Education Trust, 1998.

Connell, J. *The New Faithful: Why Young Adults are Embracing Christian Orthodoxy.* Chicago: Loyola Press, 2002.

Flanagan, K. *The Enchantment of Sociology: a Study of Theology and Culture.* London: Macmillan, 1996.

Gallagher, M.P. *Clashing Symbols: an Introduction to Faith and Culture.* London: DLT, 1997.

Goldberg, B. Bias: A CBS *Insider Exposes how the Media Distort the News* (New York: HarperCollins, 2003.

Greeley, A. *The Catholic Imagination.* U. of California Press, 2000.

Hanvey, J et al. *On the Way to Life.* Report to the Bishops of England and Wales. Catholic Education Service, 2005.

Hervieu-Léger, D. *Catholicisme, la fin d'un monde*. Paris: Bayard, 2003.

Hocken, P. *Blazing the Trail: Where is the Holy Spirit Leading the Church?* (Stoke on Trent: Alive Publishing, 2001.

Holmes, T. *Changed: Stories of God's Power to Change Lives*. Stoke on Trent: Alive Publishing, 2005.

Ker, I. *The Catholic Revival in English Literature: 1845-1961*. Leominster: Gracewing, 2003.

Knights, P. and Murray, A. *Evangelisation in England and Wales, a Report to the Catholic Bishops*. London: Catholic Communications Network, 2002.

Kreeft, P. *How to Win the Culture War: a Christian Battle Plan for a Society in Crisis*. Inter-Varsity Press, 2002.

Marchessault, G. *Médias et Foi Chrétienne: l'Image à l'épreuve de l'Idolatrie*. Novalis, 1998.

Marco, D. de and Wiker, B. *Architects of the Culture of Death*. San Francisco: Ignatius Press, 2004.

Martin, R. *The Catholic Church at the End of an Age*. San Francisco: Ignatius Press, 1994.

Martin, R. and Williamson, P. (eds) *Pope John Paul II and the New Evangelization*. San Francisco: Ignatius Press, 1995.

Nichols, A. *Christendom Awake: on Re-energising the Church in Culture*. Edinburgh: T&T Clark, 1999.

Pearce, J. *Literary Giants; Literary Catholics*. San Francisco:Ignatius Press, 2005.

Plunkett, D. *Heaven Wants to be Heard*. Leominster:

Gracewing, 1997.

Plunkett, D. 'The New Evangelisation of Peoples and Cultures' in John Redford, ed. *Hear O Islands: Theology and Catechesis for the new Millennium.* Dublin: Veritas, 2002.

Pollard, N. *Why do they do that? Understanding Teenagers.* Oxford: Lion Publishing, 1998

Rizzi, A. *The Science Before Science: A Guide to Thinking in the 21st Century.* Bloomington: Authorhouse Press, 2004.

Robinson, J. *The Inner Goddess: Feminist Theology in the Light of Catholic Teaching.* Leominster: Gracewing, 1998.

Saward, J. *The Beauty of Holiness and the Holiness of Beauty.* San Francisco: Ignatius Press, 1997.

Scruton, R. *An Intelligent Person's Guide to Modern Culture.* London: Duckworth, 1998.

Tincq, H. and Defois, G. *Les Médias et l'Eglise: Evangélisation et Information: le Conflit de deux Paroles.* Paris: CFPJ Editions, 1997.

Viladesau, R. *Theology and the Arts: Encountering God through Music, Art and Rhetoric.* New York: Paulist Press, 2000.

Wiker, B. and Witt, J. *A Meaningful World: How the Arts and Sciences Reveal the Genius of Nature.* Westmont, Ill., InterVarsity Press, 2006.

Internet

www.alphacourse.org ; www.alphacourse.org/catholics; www.alphacourse.org/youth are official website pages of Alpha, the worldwide evangelism course developed by the Church of England at Holy Trinity Brompton church, London.

www.caseresources.org.uk; www.life4seekers.co.uk are websites maintained by the Catholic Agency to Support Evangelisation (CASE), an organisation set up by the Bishops of England and Wales.

www.catholicevangel.org, a website set up by Catholic Evangelisation Services in England with information about video and training resources offered.

www.christlife.org, website of the Baltimore Diocese for evangelisation, renewal and Christian unity, with links to a range of American organisations with a concern for evangelisation.

www.communio-irc.com, website of Communio, the international theological journal founded by the then Cardinal Ratzinger

www.crisismagazine.com is a website linked to a journal that offers a wide-ranging selection of articles on cultural and religious issues.

www.ewtn.com, the website of The Eternal Word Network,

provides not only details of their television and radio programming but of the documentary and spiritual support services they offer, in which evangelisation is a major focus.

www.ktotv.com, website of the French Catholic television station that features the evangelising of culture and associated spiritual themes.

www.maryvale.ac.uk, website of the Maryvale Institute and giving details of its philosophy and courses in Theology and Catechetics.

www.staustinreview.com, website of the St Austin Review, an international review of Christian culture, literature and ideas.

www.secondspring.co.uk, website of the G.K.Chesterton Institute for Faith and Culture

www.vatican.va is the official website of the Vatican through which all its services and departments can be reached and key Church documents downloaded.

www.youth2000.org, a website to introduce the worldwide organisation for young Catholics that has been active in evangelisation among youth, in World Youth Days and local prayer groups.

www.zenit.org, website that offers an up-to-date news service, often carrying the text of papal and other speeches by senior Church officials.